THE MILFORD SERIES

Popular Writers of Today

VOLUME NINE

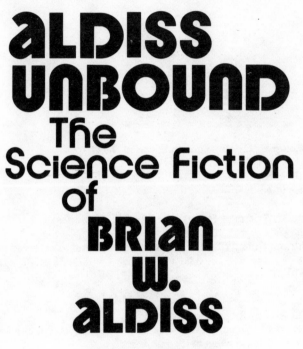

aLDISS UNBOUND
The Science Fiction of BRian W. aLDISS

Richard Mathews

R. REGINALD

THE 𝕭𝖔𝖗𝖌𝖔 𝕻𝖗𝖊𝖘𝖘

SAN BERNARDINO, CALIFORNIA

MCMLXXVII

To Julie

Library of Congress Cataloging in Publication Data

Mathews, Richard, 1944-
    Aldiss unbound.

    (Popular Writers of Today; v. 9) (The Milford Series)
    Bibliography: p.
    1. Aldiss, Brian Wilson, 1925-   —Criticism and interpretation. I. Title
PR6051.L3Z78   823′.9′14   77-24582
ISBN 0-89370-213-7

Produced, designed, and published by R. Reginald, The Borgo Press, P.O.
Box 2845, San Bernardino, CA 92406. Composition by Mary A. Burgess.
Cover design by Judy Cloyd. Printed in the United States of America by
Griffin Printing & Lithograph Company, Glendale, CA.

                        First Edition————October, 1977

WHEREIN PROTEUS MEETS PROMETHEUS

Brian W. Aldiss has at least two faces; two mythic personalities meet and
erge in his writing. One conceals a shy grin, cracks jokes (just over the
ader's head, like a whip), changes expression and appearance so rapidly
at it's difficult to pin down this enigmatic character. The other face bears
noble and long-suffering gaze, full of daring knowledge, peering unflinch-
gly into secret and forbidden matters. Beyond the suffering one sees courage
these deep eyes, reflecting a personality of unchanging integrity set irrevo-
bly against the forces of entrenched tyranny.

Through the writing of fiction and nonfiction, poetry and short stories, essays
d criticism, Aldiss unites far-ranging points of view as he carries on the
adition of the man of letters. He has won awards for both his fiction and criti-
sm, and though he pushes steadily into new stylistic experiments and new
enres, he has maintained a wide popular base in England while steadily win-
ng an international audience. In 1965, writing an introduction to *Best Science
iction Stories of Brian W. Aldiss*, he explained that "it looks as if science fic-
on has grown wide enough to reach the point that ordinary fiction reached
ng ago: where it divides into highbrow and lowbrow, into popular and eso-
ric, or into sheep and goats, or however you care to phrase it. This is a
ss. . . ." Aldiss, like many of the world's best storytellers, realizes the vitality
f an undivided fiction, a fiction which looks two ways, at once popular and art-
l. One reason Aldiss is such a good writer is that he insists his two faces meet;
e includes both the sheep and the goats.

Few times in the history of Western literature have the qualities of high art
nd wide popularity managed to come together. The most splendid example
as the golden age of Greek theatre. Five centuries before Christ the Greek
laywright Aeschylus rode the crest of public acclaim, winning thirteen first-
lace prizes for his plays. One of these, *Prometheus Bound*, showed the world
e face of the Titan hero Prometheus, who dared to steal fire from the gods,
nd thereby stole power and the arts for man. For this disobedience Prometheus
lls from grace and is punished by being chained to a rock where he is tortured
y vultures gnawing everlastingly at his liver; for his challenge to authority,
e suffers alienation and great pain. Aeschylus's companion play, *Prometheus
nbound*, survives only in fragments, but the 19th century poet Shelley brought
e character to Aldiss's native soil in a lyrical poem under the same title.
 Shelley's story, Prometheus never gives in to the will of the enraged and
rannical god. Though he suffers, he learns to endure and ceases to hate
e origin of his suffering. Shelley portrays the difficult psychological process
f regeneration in which head and heart are purified through a revolutionary
ruggle. This character Prometheus, whose name means "foresighted" or
prophetic," has been associated with science fiction ever since Mary Shelley
tled her influential novel *Frankenstein; or, The Modern Prometheus*.

Another figure from the golden myths of Greece is Proteus. He is a different
rt of prophet, an 'old man of the sea' whose nature is changeable as water.
roteus has the gift of being able to alter his shape at will into an infinite variety
f appearances. A reluctant prophet, he is slippery and difficult to pin down.
e has a sly sense of humor, always playing tricks and shifting ground.

3

Brian Aldiss is a Protean prophet with Promethean tendencies.

If science fiction is dividing into the popular and esoteric, or into shee
and goats, it is clear Aldiss has chosen sides. By his very nature he finds th
boundaries of simple popularity a limitation, and clearly wishes to ventur
beyond these limits into the uncharted waters of the experimental and esoteri
Like any prophet, or any writer, he is concerned with the language he uses t
communicate—with words that shift and play games, with words that challeng
and reveal. Committed to growth and change, he also steadfastly and painful
insists on examining his own nature, his moral stature, and his place in th
universe.

The complexities and subtleties of Aldiss's work have been extremely difficu
to capture in such a brief study. He underwent a revolution in his writing abou
the time of his second marriage, and the reader may recognize in the openin
pages of this monograph the difficulty of finding a single clear direction in th
early work. The groping process lies at the heart of all creative experienc
as the writer tries to find his literary path; I re-experienced that struggle myse
in attempting to present a unified treatment of Aldiss's different faces an
phases. Suddenly, midway through, the disconnected themes and faces com
together and to life with astounding clarity. This is not, of course, the final wor
on Brian Aldiss, who continues to expand his imaginative horizons with eac
new book. But it does represent the first serious look at the man and his wo
and I hope it will stimulate further discussion on this vastly underrated autho

SINGING IN A NEW UNIVERSE

Brian W. Aldiss was born in the busy little market village of East Dereham
near Norfolk, England, in 1925. His father was a shopkeeper, but it was clear t
the son from an early age that he "was no more interested in his father's busi
ness than was Kafka in similar circumstances." The narrow horizons of th
small East Dereham universe were shattered at a tender age: "What happene
to me at eight was a terrible thing. . . . I was sent away to boarding school, an
at boarding school I remained until I was seventeen and old enough to go int
the army—whereupon I was promptly whisked abroad to the Far East for fou
years. So my severance from home and parents began early in life, far to
early." Aldiss confesses that "many years of adult life passed before I shoo
off that cold shadow of exile."

This sense of alienation lingers throughout most of his writing, a quality h
shares with James Joyce, Ernest Hemingway, and others of the "lost genera
tion." Perhaps the writer is always an exile—Joyce's work leads to this conclu
sion, and much of Aldiss's writing stresses a similar message. In any case, h
exile from home drove him more intensely into reading and writing. He rea
widely, including a great deal of early pulp science fiction, and "was foreve
making books at prep school." He became an authority on prehistoric life, an
actively pursued his interest in the sciences. He wrote ghost stories, detectiv
stories, melodrama, space stories, and even "space-pornography," as well a
keeping a voluminous diary. When he left the service in 1948, he knew h
wanted to be a writer—a poet, he thought—and he got a job in a bookstore a

4

Oxford to support himself. Here was a perfect place to come to intimate terms with the literary tradition, and he particularly immersed himself in reading Fielding, Johnson, and Sterne. At the same time, "we were always throwing out books—a useful reminder that, however successful one is, every dog has his day."

The natural affinity he felt for all aspects of the literary world led him to contribute to the trade paper, *The Bookseller*, and the editor commissioned a series in diary form about life in a pleasant but imaginary bookshop. After a favorable reception, the pieces were collected and published by Faber & Faber in 1955. The writing career of Brian Aldiss had begun. "My very first book, *The Brightfount Diaries*, is a social comedy told in diary form, where style and subject matter—mainly life in a bookshop—are closely wedded," Aldiss says in a recent letter, "so I *began* freaky." The "freakiness" of the beginning has more to do with the close wedding of form and content than with a strangeness in subject, and the marriage holds true in his later writing. Such classically bookish origins might also be freakish for a popular science fiction author. He recognized that his own artistic talents suited him for fiction, and gradually gave up his intention of becoming a poet, "persuaded by reading Eliot, Auden, MacNiece, and John Donne, who showed me what poetry really was." But even in his most fantastic novels he is always concerned with literary and artistic works.

In 1957, Faber published his remarkable first collection of short stories, *Space, Time and Nathaniel*. In his introduction to that book he explains "SF and poetry have much in common. Both have a sly, surprising music; neither are particularly easy to write." If one savors the title of this collection, most of its important themes become clear. Here for the first time we recognize the unique and challenging imagination which unwinds through countless Aldiss plots. Space and time are of paramount concern. He begins with the abstract theoretical foundations which are the assumptions behind our perceptions of reality. Added to this conceptual frame of reference is the individual perspective which gives it meaning—Nathaniel. Aldiss' world constantly stresses the limits and implications of relativity. The individual is more clearly revealed when set against the boundless perspectives of space. Science fiction was the ideal form for Aldiss, who later observes in the same introduction, "The corsets of conformity pinch on all sides." Aldiss *needs* the infinite space that science fiction allows him, and yet he continually brings us back to ponder the dignity and worthiness of a single human being.

His fascination with personal insight and character quirks adds liveliness to even the most abstract tale, and one of the strengths of these early stories is their characterizations, which are far richer than those usually encountered in the pulp fiction of those days.

Coupled with his theoretical framework of space-time continuum, and the creation of believable and rounded human characters, is Aldiss's delight and skill with literary style, with the words themselves. He purposefully enriched his writing with stylistic techniques capable of adding depth to his fiction. For example, as a gesture to the poetic career he had imagined for himself, he arranged the contents page of this first collection so that the titles of the three types of story are laid out in octet and sextet form, like a sonnet. There are fourteen titles.

Just as the universe itself is more than a random ordering of events, the well-constructed literary work contains more than a hodge-podge of scattered, isolated pieces. Aldiss's concern for structure includes both the macrocosm and microcosm, and in this group of stories he manifests his structural skill in small details (like the arrangement of the contents page) as well as in the overall progression of the stories themselves and their organization into a larger whole. The complete collection has not been printed in this country, but American readers will find many of the individual tales in two paperbacks, *Who Can Replace a Man?* and *No Time Like Tomorrow*. Among the best stories are "Dumb Show" and "The Failed Men" (also called "Ahead"). Both of these demonstrate quite clearly a multi-level awareness of structure which was part of Aldiss's science fiction from the first.

"Dumb Show" is set in a future where explosive weaponry has been replace by far more efficient ultrasonic technology. In a devastating assault by sound waves, most of the population is deafened, and those infants and children too young to have learned language are doomed to remain dumb in a silent world. In fact, one of society's problems is the large-scale effort to teach the meaning of language to future generations of mankind. The central characters are a Grandmother and her Granddaughter, one of the uneducated victims of the attack. The Grandmother carries a printed cardboard sign bearing the single word "DON'T," but the word is not really understood by the child. Most of the story explores the Grandmother's frustration at being forced to coexist and communicate with the child without the use of language. The hostilities which develop through lack of communication are presented with subtlety and insight. In a curious conclusion, a second attack is launched, with a sound wave capable of causing rapid growth and expansion. The Grandmother is intrigued by what seem to be dancing giants coming across the horizon, until she realizes suddenly that she too is growing to gigantic proportions. The story ends with the unforgettable image of the dumb Grandchild caught up in an absurdly magnified growth process for which her young cells yearn. Time and space fall away, dwarfed by the fantastic expansion of her body: "She saw the ground dwindle. She felt the warmth of the stars, the curvature of the earth." With an impulse which makes clear Aldiss's poetic sense of language, the final ambiguous paragraph is terrifyingly lyrical: "In her brain, the delighted thoughts were wasps in a honey pot; bees in a hive, flies in a chapel, gnats in a factory, midges in a Sahara, sparks up an everlasting flue, a comet falling for ever in a noiseless void, a voice singing in a new universe."

Problems of communication, and a consuming interest in language, are clearly evident in "Dumb Show," in the plot itself, in its economical style, and in the very sound-sense pun of the title. Sound and sense are also interrelated in "The Failed Men." In this study, people from the present undertake a mercy mission to the future to save the last surviving humans, the "failed men" of the title. The mission is put together by yet another future generation, one far in advance

6

of the present humanity but equally removed from the ultimate degeneration of the end. Each generation has developed its own consciousness; and great difficulties arise when present-day men attempt to speak to future members of the species, in order to find out the cause of their failings. Working through computer banks of translation machines, man tries to converse with his future self, but the failed men think only in abstractions, and it is impossible to tell from their abstract and circular responses precisely what the specifics are: "'the start determines the resolution and the finish arbitrarily determines the beginning of the case." The circularity of the response reflects the circularity of the problem itself: "You see, language is the most intrinsic product of any culture; you can't comprehend the language till you've understood the culture—and how do you understand a culture till you know its language?"

We are left with this terrible vision of the end of mankind, a race of failures burying themselves, and the children of the past digging up the men of the future (a reversal on the stereotyped image of future generations unearthing the achievements of their ancestors—a comment itself upon the historical mission of futuristic fiction): "Working day and night, we tunneled forward, furrowing up the earth as you strip back a soiled bed. In the mould, a face would appear, an arm with the long fingers, a pair of legs tumbling into the light. We would stop the machine and get down to the body, digging with trowels round it. . . . They would be in a coma. Their eyes would open, staring like peek-a-boo dolls, then close again with a click. We'd patch them up with an injection, stack them on stretchers and send them back in a load to base." There is only one word which seems to come close to a reason for the self-burial, and it is the untranslatable word "struback." Aldiss describes it in terms of pure sound, "a long hollow syllable, followed by a short click." There is something in this abstract sound which seems to echo the circular motifs spiraling throughout the story: the causes for this self-burial "strew back" into time, so that the end is the beginning. The history of mankind is perceived as "a long hollow syllable, followed by a short click" of extinction. "I turned that word over in my tired mind. Night after night," the narrator says. "It became the symbol of the Failed Men." An untranslatable word, the failure to communicate, the symbol of Failed Men. Faced with this failure, there is terrible irony in their jaded perception of time: "There's plenty of time—too much, more than anyone will ever need."

In the skillfully enigmatic stories of *Space, Time and Nathaniel*, Aldiss establishes the terrain he will explore. His concerns with space, time, individual character, growth (change), and language remain prominent throughout the rest of his writing. These two stories form only a small part of a collection which demonstrates a remarkable mastery of form, and an original discovery of worthy subjects. There is about them the excitement of a young writer discovering his voice. Aldiss has accurately remarked, "My short stories [and he has written over 150 since this collection was published] would be more widely known if I did not write novels."

7

SHORT AND SWEET

Most of Aldiss's earliest work was written in shorter forms. The stories from *Space, Time and Nathaniel* range from 2,375 words ("T") to 6,600 ("The Shub-Shub Race"). His 1958 novel *Non-Stop* (published in the U.S. as *Starship*) is really a sustained short story, despite its classification as a novel; or perhaps it comes closer to the hybrid novella format of such other 1958 pieces as "Equator" (31,000 words) and "Segregation" (17,000 words). This format was partly the influence of *New Worlds*, where most of the material originally appeared; and Aldiss was very much a part of the *New Worlds* renaissance, as he tells us in "Magic and Bare Boards" (*Hell's Cartographers*, 1975). At a time when short fiction markets were drying up, science fiction periodicals commanded an audience eager to pay for original material. All of the most exciting developments in the short story during the late '50s and throughout the '60s took place in science fiction, and Aldiss was among the groundbreakers. 1959 saw the publication of eleven new stories in *Canopy of Time* (also called *Galaxies Like Grains of Sand*). The brief novel *Bow Down to Nul*, which originally appeared in story form in *New Worlds* as "X for Exploitation," was published by Ace in 1960 (it was also issued by Digit Books as *The Interpreter*). In 1962, the novel *Hothouse* was built up from connected short stories, and the eight tales of *The Airs of Earth* (the American edition was *Starswarm*) followed in 1963. Even in the years 1964-67, though he had mastered an original novel technique quite unlike the structure of his short stories, he continued to exercise his talents in abbreviated and concise narratives. *The Dark Light Years* and *Greybeard* of 1964 are both relatively short. The compact *Earthworks* was developed out of the story "Skeleton Crew" in 1965, and 1966 saw publication of another ten-story collection, *The Saliva Tree and Other Strange Growths*. It is important to recognize Aldiss's complete mastery of the short story and novella forms. When he first discovered the French anti-novel, and fully developed his own complex novelistic structures in *Report on Probability A* (written in 1962), the book from which one can date his full emergence as a novelist, Aldiss found that the linked stories of *Hothouse* had already begun to evolve in that direction. He recognized in the French *New Novel*, particularly Robbe-Grillet's *Jealousy* and Michel Butor's *Passing Time*, the perfect direction for his own next step. His publishers didn't agree, however, and hiˉ novel didn't see print until 1968.

Publishers spoiled one dimension of *Non-Stop* when they titled the U.S. edition *Starship*, and gave away the basic twist of the plot. The book is about a community occupying unfamiliar territory, the nature and extend of which they don't understand. The members of this city-state are caught up in petty territorial conflicts and superstition until the central characters set out to explore the unknown. They finally discover they are on board a starship which has been travelling out of control for generations. Everyone has forgotten where they were going and how to navigate. There is no one at the wheel. Analogs between this ship and our real world on Spaceship Earth—both virtually leaderless and out of control—come constantly to mind while reading the book. Here is one manifestation of the "unbound" journey—the incomprehensible trip with no known destination. The multifaceted parallels are suggested in the first sentence: "Like an echo bounding from a distant object and returning to its source, the sound of Roy Complain's beating heart seemed to him to fill the clearing."

Although the novel begins with an "echo" and ends "wordlessly" as the ship breaks apart into its various decks, each deck a world of its own, the Aldissian interest in words is central. Part of the problem for the inhabitants of the space-ship-world is that their language has broken down: words have ceased to have their original meanings. Thus, place names which actually designate parts of a spacecraft have no more significance to the inhabitants of the ship than any other arbitrarily-chosen words. Only near the end of the novel do we realize that "Quarters," "Deadways," and "Forwards" are actually quite conventional ways of designating areas of a ship.

The Priest Marapper introduces the issue early in the book as he tries to explain his theory, assembled from myth, history and research, that they are in "a sort of container called a ship, moving from one bit of the world to another." "What if the world *is* called ship, or the ship the world, it makes no difference to us," Complain says. The point is, it *does* make a difference. Words are essential to understanding and communication; without words we are isolated and meaningless—our own heartbeats can seem to fill the universe. The priest preserves meaning through knowledge and belief, which add in turn a dimension of significance to his words, and cause him to *act*. He is aided primarily by another communicator, Fermour, a story-teller and poet, the type of artist-hero who appears so often in Aldiss's fiction. His tales are hopeful and exciting, especially to the children, and he uses the circle image to suggest limitless possibilities: "Now the world is a wonderful place. It is constructed of layers and layers, like this one, and these layers do not end, because they eventually turn a circle on to themselves. So you could walk on and on for ever and never reach the end of the world."

The inscription which serves as prelude to the story is from R. L. Stevenson: "To travel hopefully is a better thing than to arrive. . ." Fighting their way through the "Ponic" jungles—a term which becomes understandable when we finally realize these are simply *hydroponics*, out of control like the ship—the characters eventually do arrive at an explanation. They find they are locked in Earth orbit while scientists look for a way to counteract a cellular mutation inflicting the voyagers. At the book's end, though the priest and the artist have led the way to hope, it is the simpler characters—Complain and Vyann—who seem to benefit from it most. Earth orbit—another circle which turns in upon itself—is to these innocents a knowledge filled with possibiltiy: "Neither of them had even been really sure of what it was they wanted: so they, after all, had been the ones most likely to find it." They have companionship and new hope; that is all they need.

Equator reveals multiple dimensions of meaning in the pun of its title. It refers first to the setting—torrid, tropical, jungle land near Sumatra, a landscape which has strong personal appeal for Aldiss, and which returns as the setting for *A Rude Awakening*, the third of his Horatio Stubbs novels. "In the tropics, nothing was itself," Aldiss tells us on the first page, "merely fabric stretched over heat, poses over pulses.'' An equation suggests that one thing is not only equal to itself, but equal to other factors as well; here it is impossible to tell Roskian spacemen from third world natives, truth from lies, friend from foe. The atmosphere in the city is ominous: ''The feeling that something gigantic might happen any day hovered over its hot, scented streets.''

On one level, the book is a spy or detective story, with the hero, Tyne Leslie, trying to sort out truth from deception. Roskian aliens from Alpha Centauri II have established an Earth base near the equator. Tyne, Allan Cunliffe, and Murray Mumford are on a spy patrol when they are caught by the Rosks. Tyne is wounded, Allan apparently killed, and Tyne and Murray escape to report what they can. Slowly Tyne realizes he is not getting accurate reports from Murray and his superiors, and sets out on his own to unravel what really happened. From Rosk double-agent Benda Ittai, Tyne learns that Murray has been carrying a microfilm containing ''a complete record of the imminent invasion of Earth by an Alpha fleet.'' Tyne then becomes the equator in a balancing act to avert such a catastrophe; he believes he is the only man on earth who realizes what is at stake.

Events in the book weigh individual human actions against planetary cataclysms, and establish a clear relationship between the microcosm (microfilm) and macrocosm (interplanetary invasion). It turns out that Tyne is not alone in feeling a sense of urgent moral responsibility. The hopeful message of the book is that morality is a concern of all conscious beings, directly related to accurate communication. ''Our people are as human as yours,'' Benda explains. ''Please see this terrible business as a moral struggle rather than a detective game. When their eyes are opened to what is going on behind their backs, all my people will surely rise.'' Benda's people have apparently lost their perspective, like the ship's passengers in *Non-Stop*: ''We were all born on the ship, thinking ourselves colonists. There must have been sealed orders (invasion plans) passed down from one generation of the officer class to the next.''

Early in the book, Tyne formulates a ''Theory of Irresponsible Activity,'' which allows him to ignore the real implications of his actions. Events cause him to reverse his position. The turning point in his moral recognition occurs within the crumbling framework of the old religious system: ''They emerged into a secluded courtyard surrounded by small cells once inhabited by novices. The whole place was slowly crumbling; it might have been built of old bread.'' Despite the crumbling moral structure, communication (hence, communion) is still possible—and it can still be accomplished by individuals willing to seize, like Prometheus, the power from the tyrants: ''The leaders plotted, and the rest followed like sheep—unless they could be roused to see that only muttonhood awaited them.''

The end of the novel is not without irony; the threat is revealed as a bluff. Even with the final reversal, individual worth remains intact. Tyne cannot comprehend the psychology of power: ''Frustratedly, he turned to Benda Ittai. Here at least was someone worth trying to comprehend. . . . She smiled at him. It was a very comprehensible smile.''

The setting, themes and image patterns of ''Segregation'' nicely complement

10

nd amplify *Equator*. While not as rich a story, "Segregation" is nonetheless entertaining and intriguing, and an especially good companion piece. There are common images of heat and cold in both, and even the openings are complementary; *Equator* starts at "the one time of day when you could almost feel the world rotating," and "Segregation" opens "At other times of day." The setting for 'Segregation" is another "equatorial zone" where "the surrounding jungle grew thickly." As we would expect, communication is the central problem. Interplanetary investigators (PEST—Planetary Ecological Survey Team) try to make sense of segregated races on a planet where a nearly-senile missionary is the only one capable of "understanding the language and situation."

The story is resolved by a simplified explanation of a puzzling situation. The implications seem less satisfying than in Aldiss's best writing, but there is one passage worth quoting as part of the motivation for the SF artist. In a moment of candor, the missionary, Dangerfield suggests, "Everyone who goes into space has a good reason driving them. . . you don't only need escape velocity, you need a private dream—or a private nightmare." Aldiss's space fiction is not escape, nor is it based primarily on "good reason." For this modern Romantic, the dream is necessary to give reason significance: "It is safer for a novelist to choose as his subject something he feels. . . than something he knows about."

THE COMMUNION OF LAUGHTER

The series of communication novellas concludes with *The Interpreter* (1960) also called *Bow Down to Nul*), and *The Primal Urge* (1961). *The Interpreter* shows us the consequences of manipulative exploitation of communication channels; in *Urge*, Aldiss satirizes the attempt to provide "authentic" communication by plugging technology directly into the brain's unconscious impulses. Satire in the latter novel is also indicative of an evolution in Aldiss's writing techniques and thematic material. Initially approaching his themes from a serious perspective, he now probes and crossexamines the motifs until he begins to develop a self-consciously ironic appreciation for his own intensity; suddenly he turns what were serious stylistic questions into humorous entertainment. The ability to laugh at oneself is, after all one of the most graceful of human traits.

The cover of the Digit Book edition of *The Interpreter* bills it as "A Story of Devilry and Corruption in a Fantastic Galctic Empire of Tomorrow." This is not completely wrong, but the "Devilry" of the novel is misleading. The forces of evil are shown to lurk within individual minds, and within the corruptible and artificial systems imagined and created by those minds. The central figure of this novel is Earthman Gary Towler, chief interpreter for the apparently corrupt and tyrannical Nuls. The book calls into sharp focus the pivotal importance of the individual, for Towler is able to conduct himself as a powerful third force in the dialectic of intergalactic forces.

In his continuing explorations of the powers and functions of language, Aldiss treats both the external effects of communication—as evident, for instance in "Dumb Show," or the circumstances of *Non-Stop*—and the internal basis for communication: "Thought. Thought: that field of force still to be analysed. Thought: as inseparable from a higher being as gravity from a planet." It is not as if he has divorced language and communication from thought in his earlier published books, but here he specifically moves to explore the internal mental landscape from the very first sentence. The first-person narrator—the Nul Wattol Forlie—speaks in the opening pages, putting us close to the individual consciousness, and revealing the interior distances between characters. Thought is as necessary to proper performance of a translator's functions as idea or theme is necessary to successful fiction. The thoughtful problem-ridden translator of "The Failed Men" is fleshed out in another guise in "The Interpreter," and one can almost hear Aldiss himself in the "I" of th book: "Thought. . . . It wraps around me, as my senses go about their endless job of turning all the external world into symbols." The issue is clear from the start: "I can know no external thing without its being touched—perhaps in some unguessable way transmuted—by my thought. . . was it real, or a mis interpretation in my mind." Even the physical perspective of this Nul reminds us of Aldiss's technique as a writer: "I lie flat on the wide wall by the old har bour, gazing up at the universe." Like the best authors of fantastic fiction Aldiss succeeds in treating convincing action in a vast universe by making the familiar objects—single characters, or a comfortably recognizable old wall by a harbor—reassuringly present to lend an air of authenticity and reality to the fiction.

Like many of Aldiss's most "advanced" aliens, the Nuls are larger than men with an external appearance at once unhuman and unrevealing. The description of the Commissioner Par-Chavorlem is typical: he is ten feet tall, immensely solid and "almost cylindrical, except for his arms and legs. A Nul was like a canister to which two three-armed starfish were joined, one at the base, forming legs, one midway up, forming arms. . . . Near the top of his cylindrical body were three regularly spaced eye-stalks, while on top of his 'head' was the usua fleshy comb. All his other features were concealed under the wide flaps of his arms; his mouth, his olfactory nerves, his aural cavities, his reproductive or gans. A Nul was a secret creature whose exterior betrayed very little." (The dif ferences between external appearance and internal reality are similarly explored in *The Dark Light Years*.) Aldiss doubly points out the disjunctures between planetary races when he shifts point-of-view, showing us the Nul Signatory encountering a human for the first time: "It was chiefly a moral shock. These terrestrials had their private features, their mouths and other orifices, promi nently on display, in a manner distasteful to him."

The signatory (Synvoret), like Towler, is essentially after the truth, but recog nizes that it is "notoriously an illusive thing." Typical of the running philo sophical commentary which fills Aldiss's works, the Signatory reflects, "In a complex universe, truth like time might be both subjective and objective, with no reconciliation possible." It is the task of Towler to weather his own "moral confusion," to decide how much his "translations" (reports) to Synvoret giving the situation on Earth, will cover up the actual situation. In an atmo sphere where it is impossible to fix any reliable point of trust, the decision to communicate honestly becomes incredibly difficult. Finally, when Towler de cides to offer what he hopes is positive proof of the corrupt regime on earth, he finds that even physical evidence can be misinterpreted. At the last moment, he attempts to kill the emissary and sabotage the investigative mission. Though that attempt fails, it clearly crystalizes Towler's moral position.

The corrupt government of Par-Chavorlem is replaced for all the wrong reasons. Instead of withdrawing it for the fierce tyranny it has inflicted, the authorities replace the government for being altogether too lax. It is undoubtedly a happy ending, but one which leaves cause and effect very much in doubt. Towler's reactions take him into a realm of feeling and thought beyond language: "His face relaxed and he began to laugh, partly from the irony of it, partly from sheer lightheartedness. There was no word for how he felt, either in his own tongue or in Partussian." Whether or not the moral struggle and decisiveness or Towler have *caused* the happy ending, forces far beyond the scope of a single human being have brought it about, and the fact that this happiness developed through an ironic joke does not prevent the great catharsis: "It was as if a great purgative merriment had seized the whole ancient town before sweeping out until its last ripples reached the last corners of the globe." Aldiss, at the end of a very intense and traumatic struggle, turns to humor for a resolving and integrative communication. The communion of laughter unites humanity as practically no other communication can: "In the bright sunlight, it was as if everyone was suddenly laughing."

Through the Nul Wattol Forlie on the first page of the novel, Aldiss says, "I have no cause for optimism, yet I am optimistic." The human face relaxing at the end of this novel marks a significant progression in narrative technique. Aldiss is still grappling with the moral issues in an intense and probing manner. Like Joyce's Stephen Daedalus, he feels compelled "to forge in the smithy of his soul the uncreated conscience of his race." The creation of conscience, however, is shown to be more important than any specific actions which result from; it, for the matrix of events in the universe seems to be influenced more by accident than intent. *Bow Down to Nul* is the best of the three titles under which this book has appeared. It captures the ironic tone of the ending, being on one level a command to bow down to the creatures, the Nuls, but also labelling those creatures exactly for what they are: valueless, amounting to nothing. It also gives us a Promethean directive: bow down to nothing!

Clearly, those who have power at the top are able to nullify the actions of those at the bottom; we witness a similar interplay between power politics and individual will in *The Primal Urge*. More strongly than any of the earlier novels, *Urge* juxtaposes the primal and futuristic, using irony and humor to make a delightful game of the whole situation. Aldiss's light-handed "Author's Note" is an apology for using real people (like Aldous Huxley) and real brand-names (like Kosset Carpets) in what is obviously a piece of fiction, one not "really" about modern-day Britain ("Even the weather is too good to be true"). The settings for most of his earlier fiction are far from home, but this location is at "once unreal and typically English." Why has this reality suddenly moved so close to what we recognize?

We can know little of what Aldiss *intended* to accomplish in the shift, but we can discuss the effects. In the first place, he was attempting something new in style and tone, something fresh in science fiction. Behind this novel is the special tradition of English satire. It is part of a widely shared pleasure in tongue-in-cheek extravagance which runs from Jonathan Swift through Evelyn Waugh (*The Loved One*) to Anthony Burgess and Brian Aldiss. The closest parallels to this mode of science fiction are Orwell's *Animal Farm*, and Burgess's *The Eve of St. Venus*—in fact, Burgess and Aldiss have many things in common as contemporary writers of English science fiction, including the British touch for satire, and a passionate influence from James Joyce. There are similar elements in Orwell's *1984* or Huxley's *Brave New World*, but Aldiss hits closer to home with this double satire touching Britain's economic doldrums, the new permissiveness and the functions of power in the welfare state's relations with its public and foreign nations. In the ironic frame of mind, it is difficult to see clearly just what the primal urge is: sex or power, passion or reason, body or soul.

Part One of the book is called "A Putative Utopia" ("putative" means simply "reputed" or "supposed"). The supposition concerns a new bequest to the British public from the Ministry of Health—a disc implanted in the middle of the forehead which glows pink whenever the subconsicous is sexually aroused. While the book is a wide-ranging social satire, it focuses primarily on the disc's impact upon a single character, James Solent, and the small world around him. There is a constant trading-off between the broader social perspective and Solent's experiences, which both mirror the generalities and contradict them. Aldiss employs this as a structural device. The first section tells how Solent has the disc installed, how it glows pink when he gets together with an attractive woman. A glorious one-night stand follows, but Solent suffers the consequences—a *punitive* utopia.

Aldiss seems to have enjoyed writing this novel more than any of the previous ones. It fails to work in several places, not being as concise and forceful as the finely wrought stories; but it is filled with graceful and laughable touches. As Aldiss himself said in commenting on another SF writer's work, it "is not so much traditional SF as a story which takes SF for granted and uses its vocabulary." The only real science-fictional element in the book is the ERs (Emotinal Registers), or Norman Lights, as the discs (slightly smaller than a penny) are called. Sociologists expect the discs to revolutionize the repressed British citizens, "because they enable the id for the first time to communicate direct, without the intervention of the ego. The human ego for generations has been growing swollen at the expense of the id, from which all true drives spring." The ERs will put man in touch with the deepest centers of creativity, while providing a major new national industry. Jimmy Solent is quick to follow the lead of his flashing pink forehead, and after a wonderfully awkward bout with a liberated lady named (of course) Rose, Jimmy buys the prime ministerial hoopla, and through this single escapade believes he has discovered that "Truth lay buried in the body and could only be reached as Jimmy had reached it last night. The plunge was what absolutely must be taken. And though one had wings, the dive into the burning lake was necessary for life."

The frivolous veneer is laid over a continual reference to the culture of the present and past, particularly the literary culture. Jimmy himself, in assessing his condition, is forced to recall St. Augustine, Victorianism, and contemporary literature: "He recalled all the modern novels he had consumed in which passion was shown as a dark destroyer or, at best, as a parched desert. How crudely those authors had misread." And Jimmy is taken by his brother to one of the hottest literary theatrical hits of the season, a new Thyroid Annerson play, "No Anchorage But Ithaca," at the stumer Theatre where Odysseus and Circe banter inconsequently. Jimmy in fact is in charge of exhibitions for the IBA, the International Book Association. Mottoes from the founder adorn the walls of his office building, and as one passes from the glass doors into the foyer one reads "Only books stand between us and the cave." Despite his employment by the book industry, Jimmy makes it clear that he has no real connection to literary tradition. Only the opponents of ERs pay homage to old-fashioned literacy; the Opposition's chief leader, Bourgoyne, expresses the conservative view of progress: "It is an insult to expect a man or a woman to have a tin badge welded to his or her forehead. It's shameful! It is a descent into savagery. Soon we shall be issued with rings to go through our noses." This is one of the examples of the playful Aldissian notion that time is really flowing backward, an idea which is more fully developed in a later book.

Not only is Jimmy at the mercy of the political and economic forces which ordain that he must be equipped with an ER, he is also a victim of the physical universe, including the physical and emotional ebb and flow of his own body. "He knew little about his own physiology," Aldiss tells us. "He knew even less of the grey and beautiful world of sub-atomic particles which, as Heisenberg's Uncertainty Relation first implied, served him with thought and direction, apparently for its own inscrutably purposes. Worse still, Jimmy was content to know nothing of these things. Such control as he possessed over himself was limited; like a popular daily newspaper, he was largely at the mercy of his circulation." At the beginning of the novel Jimmy is clearly immature and ignorant. He faces a rude awakening when he finds his lovely Rose has thorns. thorns.

"You gave me so much," Jimmy tells her, speaking of their passionate night of lovemaking on the dirty boards, "I'd hoped I gave you something in return. It's hard for me to say this, but you—you were so *eager* that night."

"You didn't give me a thing," she replies.

It isn't the id which comes into play here; it's the ego. And only through his wounded ego does Jimmy have a chance to advance in understanding or humanity. Rose, his liberated Beatrice, is a fully-realized female character, one of the most convincing in Aldiss's canon. She comes off particularly well in the scene at the end of Part I where the above exchange occurs. Their final separation is wonderfully well developed: "Rose stood, as a man might have done. When she looked into his eyes, Jimmy was again baffled; something of her expression, either in the translucent world of her pupils or in the set of her face, offered him courage. It was as if she silently said, 'Life is hell, brother; that's a knowledge we both share,' but Jimmy was too inexperienced to know that looks convey unmistakeably what language cannot."

Part II of the book, "Browbeaten but Victorious," leaps and hops more vigorously over the lively cast of characters, and centers less on Jimmy himself than on the madcap intrigues of his society. Rose, it seems, is the inventor of the ERs. The merry chase leads through city and country all around this "brash new world," and the whole trip is lightly sprinkled with literary puns. A chapter called "The Light That Failed" casts the shadow of Kipling across the ER discs, and Shakespeare is made to justify science fiction: "This is an art, which does mend nature, change it rather; but the art itself is nature." Jimmy, though his job is selling books, must still try to come to terms with his reality. Books begin to creep increasingly into his frame of reference: "He sat at his desk in a brown study, the sound of traffic coming to him like Matthew Arnold's melancholy, long, withdrawing roar." The hectic traffic of London becomes symbolic of the amazing tangle of intrigues which comprise the operations of modern society, a symbol which is used to conclude the book. Shakespeare takes center stage again as the first lady of the Theatre condemns the glowing discs: "We come not to praise drama but to bury it. Its death is our death. How can we any longer face the footlights when from Monday on all of us will wear headlights? Equipped with a flashing disc, would King Lear have the power to make us weep?. . .No, my friends, we are cut off from our past by the Emotion Register. . . . The modern world has finally eclipsed all that was good or valuable. Therefore we weep today, and on this ancient and honoured body I do not throw rosemary—that's for remembrance."

Aldiss's ending is something out of the Keystone cops, featuring "Hot Pursuits and Cold Shoulders." At long last, little Jimmy finds an ordinary girl (Alyson), and: "Optimism crawled aphrodisiac-wise through his arteries, surprising him by its presence." The only thing which averts discomania is the discovery that Rose had planned to follow up her marketing of the pink lights with little green ones that light up when you tell a lie. Fortunately, the government arranges for her abduction by the Russians. The lie-revealing discs would have "meant a death blow to British diplomacy." United with his safe and ordinary girl, arm in arm, Jimmy and Alyson walk out "into the London air, evening-calm, gasoline-sweet." Like the final word, "gasoline-sweet," the whole novel is a piece of technological confection, but it once again affirms an instinctive optimism which surges through Aldiss's own *art*eries, and, in a delightfully entertaining manner, loosens the author's language sense to embrace some fantastic constructions: "Silence burst over them like an exploding muffin." The playful style of this book is an obvious proving ground for *Report on Probability A* and *Barefoot in the Head*; in fact, there is an actual *Barefoot* footprint here, with the silent receptionist in Jimmy's office, Mrs. Charteris (Charteris is *Head*'s hero).

Before leaving the short, sweet pieces which form a minor group unto themselves, we should give some fuller consideration to the stories which are included in : *Galaxies Like Grains of Sand* (1960), *Starswarm* (1964), and *Who Can Replace a Man?* (1967). One influence which becomes increasingly clear in a reading of Aldiss is the impact, especially on his short stories, of Edgar Allen Poe. The history of science fiction which Aldiss published in 1973,

Billion Year Spree, devotes an entire chapter to Poe. Aldiss calls him the "Hamlet of letters," and quotes with approval a journal entry for 1856 from the Brothers Goncourt: "After reading Edgar Allen Poe. Something the critics have not noticed: a new literary world, pointing to the literature of the twentieth century. Scientific miracles, fables, on the pattern A + B; a clear-sighted, sickly literature. . . . Things playing a more important part than people; love giving way to deductions and other sources of ideas, style, subject and interest; the basis of the novel transferred from the heart to the head, from the passion to the idea, from the drama to the denouement." This states the case strongly—astoundingly strongly when one considers the date—and surely Aldiss cannot be seen merely as a modern Poe. For one thing, Poe is a master of the macabre, and Aldiss obviously is not. Rather than adopting the message of Poe, Aldiss has utilized many of his unsettling techniques to provide a kindlier resolution. It is the "aphrodesiac optimism" in his veins, perhaps.

The strength in Poe's writing which Aldiss particularly applauds is an asset which he adopts for his own: "It is Poe's especial merit—shared with few other writers—that when he is at his best he threatens us with something in which, being ultimately undefined, a part of us must compulsively believe. The resolution of the story leaves that belief intact." This insight is one which strengthens the technique of all of Aldiss's early fiction. His conclusions never alleviate the questions of his stories; the reader still bears the burden of a central threat unanswered, as in his title, "Who Can Replace a Man?"

Because of variations in publishing practices, it is practically impossible to make unified sense of Aldiss's various collections of short stories. *No Time Like Tomorrow*, an American edition, contains only 6 of the 14 stories in *Space, Time and Nathaniel*, but the work represented there is among his earliest writing, stories first published 1955-1958. *Galaxies Like Grains of Sand* is a second collection of early stories, all of these published first in 1957-58. *Who Can Replace a Man?* is a wider-ranging collection which includes 5 stories from *Space, Time and Nathaniel* ("Dumb Show" is the only one not in *No Time Like Tomorrow*), plus other assorted stories published between 1955-1965. *Starswarm* includes material published between 1958-63, and has an early version of "Segregation" titled "The Game of God."

Most skillfully executed are the tales in *No Time Like Tomorrow* and *Who Can Replace a Man?* These are collections of multi-faceted stories with common thematic motifs, each maintaining its own integrity. In both *Starswarm* and *Galaxies Like Grains of Sand*, Aldiss, either at the instigation of his American publisher (Signet), or perceiving the common elements in his tales, has bound them together with a linked narrative commentary which is distracting and artificial. The running narration of the bridge material spoils the individual character of the stories, and by trying to unify them artificially, Aldiss has only placed them like fine diamonds in overly ornate settings: the conspicuous surrounding prevents a clear view of the stones.

The best practitioners of SF short story construction have created innovations in two directions: they have developed forms in which traditional demands of characterization can be flagrantly violated in favor of strong imaginative action

17

and theme, with thematic material often incorporated in a manner which earlier would have been found more appropriate to the essay than to fiction; and, they have enlarged the conception of setting and space to include interior space, exploring psychological space in geographical narrative terms which unite what might be called "stream of consciousness" techniques with intensely involving narrative story lines to create curious crossbreeds and hybrids.

Though Aldiss has stories which explore both terrains, he has made particular contributions to expanding SF possibilities interiorly. When these efforts first reached public attention in the mid-1960's, along with those of other British SF writers, the movement came to be know collectively as the "New Wave." Although this term has been overworked, it is still useful as a designation of the new narrative approach to stream-of-consciousness fiction, an approach which makes an interior wave in Aldiss's best short stories. The wave comes in on the tide of a new sea discovered by the three authors of short fiction who seem to be obvious influences on Aldiss: Poe, Kafka and Joyce. From Poe he inherits the ability to center fiction on mystery, particularly on abnormal perspectives and situations, containing the whole within an ironically rational point of view. From Kafka, Aldiss has adopted the habit of writing in realistic universals. Often, the realities of Aldiss's fiction are achieved not through details of setting or character, but through the contact with convincing universals: a form of symbolic writing, close to allegory, in which characters and incidents seem to take on the quality of symbols for less tangible forces and principles. While Kafka explored the similarity between man and animals or insects, Aldiss carries this a step forward by comparing man to vegetables and machines. Like Kafka, he is concerned with individual man's relationship to large and intricate systems—governments, bureaucracies, armies, and so forth. From Joyce he adopts a great sensitivity to, and playfulness with, language and sound, the interior monologue (which Aldiss blends with active narration and dialogue), and the story moment referred to in Joyce's works as "epiphany," a sudden, central flash of understanding that bursts upon a reader, not in a climax of action, but of consciousness. In addition, he provides from book to book an evolving portrait of an artist, and attempts to unify morality, theology, and art.

HEAT, COLD AND OTHER DICHOTOMIES

In 1962 Aldiss published what some critics still regard as his most important work, *Hothouse*. Sections of the book had already appeared in various periodicals, but the finished novel achieves a whole much greater than any of the parts. The successful wedding of these smaller units into a unified creation shows great structural skill, and a significant advance over his thematically-assembled short story collections. *Hothouse* documents a progression from Blakean innocence through experience to a higher experience. By turns, it denies and then affirms individual experience; but it remains primarily a novel of opposing cosmic forces rather than a story of an individual character. In fact, Aldiss makes a point of this, particularly in the earlier parts of the novel, where he builds sympathy for a string of individual characters, only to kill them off immediately.

This repeated plot device gradually brings home both the distinct individuality of life, and the universal principle of arbitrary death. Exercising his ironic sense of time, Aldiss begins the novel in the far future, with a primitive race of tiny humans in a vegetable world which seems at first more primeval than modern. The thrust of the tale, with its quest-structure, is to delineate a world of dichotomies taking the form of numerous either/or choices: life vs. death, good vs. evil, mind vs. body, animal vs. vegetable, heat vs. cold, light vs. dark; and, having established these dichotomies, to explore the middle ground, the area where one becomes the other, where life becomes death or the past becomes the future. It is no accident that so much of the crucial action near the end of the novel takes place in that no man's land of gray between the unfailingly dark and the eternally light parts of this futuristic world. Nor is it an accident that Gren opts at the end of the book to remain where he was born, having come through his learning process to know it more fully and love it more deeply.

The first complete American edition of *Hothouse* was not published until 1976, when Gregg Press reprinted the original English version, adding an excellent introduction by Joseph Milicia. The American paperback edition was titled *The Long Afternoon of Earth*, an abridged version which lost much of the strength of the full novel. Milicia points out in his introduction to the Gregg edition that *Hothouse* is cast in the traditional form of an odyssey, and though he does not follow the implications of this observation as far as he might, it remains a very perceptive one. There are innumerable parallels with Homer's tale, and the ironies and correspondences would be rich territory for critical investigation. On the other hand, Aldiss's hero is physically inconspicuous compared to Odysseus; and the nature of the forces that threaten him are not as simply overcome as those weathered by Odysseus, since reason is often an imappropriate means of solving crises here. Also, the vegetative universe is a different sort of opposition than the gods and creatures who oppose and delay Odysseus. But perhaps the most significant difference between the two heros is that Odysseus has a clear purpose in mind from the start of his journey: to return home to Ithaca. Gren can have no such determination, though he does in fact return home. The modern sensibility and verbal techniques are closer to Joyce than Homer, making the book a kind of interplanetary *Ulysses*.

Stylistically, Aldiss uses a beautifully shifting form, imitating the shifting realities of the novel, and the gradually maturing consciousness of Gren. The book begins simply, almost as a child's story, with uncomplicated thoughts and direct action. By the end of the book, we have moved through two very complex cerebral organisms, the morel and Sodal Ye. Form imitates content in an altogether pleasing manner.

Not only is the temporal setting confused, with the far future resembling the remote past, but images of time and comments upon it are abundant within the book. At the beginning of the novel, time is running fast, life and death occur rapidly, the older generation moves on to the "True World" of the Moon, and the younger generation, Gren among them, is left to carry on the future on Earth. The Earth and Moon are linked by traversers (giant spiders), and both spheres are part of a solar system which seems to be caught up in "that antique symbol of neglect, a spider's web." The condition of Lily-yo and the senior citizens of *Hothouse* is typical of all the heroic forces in the novel: "they journeyed, nervous, lost, in pain, knowing neither where they were nor why they were." The earth has been overtaken by growth, the light portion of it filled by a single tree (here and there are suggestions of another myth—Yggdrasill, the world tree of Norse saga). The tiny humans are the last surviving animals in a vegetable kingdom which dwarfs them, even sending the giant vegetable Traversers on their spider-like webs to populate the Moon. An early passage in the novel describes this greenhouse process: "They grew. Stunted and ailing in the beginning, they grew. With vegetal tenacity, they grew. They exhaled. They spread. They thrived. Slowly the broken wastes of the moon's lit face turned green. In the craters creepers began to flower. Up the ravaged slopes the parsleys crawled. As the atmosphere deepened, so the magic of life intensified, its rhythm strengthened, its tempo increased." The magic of life is a pervasive wonder of the book.

The early portions of the novel reflect an innocence never allowed Odysseus, and one difficult to portray convincingly in fiction. About a third of the way into the narrative, however, we begin to depart from this pre-lapsarian paradise, and the ironies involved in this state of "innocence." Part I ends with a "fall" into generation, and the comparison with Eden becomes explicit. Gren has fallen victim to the parasitic morel, a fungus which attaches itself to the head of the host and which possesses rational intelligence. (In fact, the morel later claims it was originally the *cause* of intelligence in humans). The promise of the fungus is like that of the snake: "Your eyes shall be opened. Why—you'll be like gods!" Gren's female companion, Poyly, is also contaminated with the gruesome plant; then, "Like another Eve, she drew Gren to her. They made love in the warm sunlight, letting their wooden souls fall as they undid their belts." The last sentence of the section is marvelously ambiguous: "Hand in hand, they walked together towards that way out of Nomansland, their dangerous Eden."

After this turning point, the references to time become increasingly frequent and explicit. "The morel fungus," we find, "had specialized in intelligence—the sharp and limited intelligence of the jungle." Just how limited and jungle-like its attitudes are, is slowly revealed as its hold on Gren increases, and its cruelty becomes manifest. Nonetheless, the fungus accomplishes something tangibly new in the novel: "The life forms of the great hothouse world lived out their days in ferocity or flight, pursuit or peace, before falling to the green and forming compost for the next generation. For them there was no past and no future; they were like figures woven into a tapestry, without depth. The morel, tapping human minds, was different. It had perspective." The image of the tapestry is repeated in Aldiss's more recent book, *The Malacia Tapestry*, and the sense of perspective gained by increments in intelligence and consciousness, as well as from awareness of relativity, is, as we have already seen, a major theme of Aldiss's work. The association between time and conscious thought is made directly: "Again the clocks of intelligence begin to chime." "Hear the clocks chime!" twangs the morel. "They chime for us, children!"

(The line directly echoes John Donne's phrase from his *Devotions*, which Hemingway borrowed as a title, *For Whom the Bell Tolls*.) The burden of the morel's mental challenge is very difficult for the pair to bear, and they are disoriented by this notion of perspective. Driven by the fungus to seek new lands, they have been buffeted about on the sea, and finally come to rest on an unknown island. Poyly has been joined at this point by Yattmur, and the two of them are completely disoriented by a gigantic cliff, since they have never seen one before. It appears to them that the mass is moving, falling onto them, until they only recognize at the morel's prodding, that it is merely clouds moving behind the mountain which make the cliff itself appear to move. "It is a magic cliff. It always falls, yet it never falls," Yattmur says.

The cliff becomes important for another reason. It is part of the book's ending, one of the centers for "devolving" vegetal population; the green emission of life energy is being beamed to other parts of the solar system from a dying Earth. Within a cave in this cliff Gren experiences something like an acid trip, an uncanny piece of writing that closely evokes mystical experience, overwhelming even the rationality of the morel. Aldiss links abstract and concrete impressions in such a way that the words constantly seem to mean more than they say, implying something just beyond our grasp. It is characteristic of Aldiss to include not only mind-boggling visions of space and time, but also an unparaphrastic dimension of experience which can only be labeled mystical. This vision is yet another reality, a true and intense one, and comprises one of the most glorious of human capabilities, a brief glimpse of universal unity and eternity. Aldiss may have attempted a paraphrase of this mystical perception through his awareness of the drug experience—hallucinaton was another dimension associated with the New Wave—but it remains for Aldiss, more than any of the other writers of the '60s and '70s, to make the profound connections between such experience, the scientific understanding of Heisenberg and Einstein, and the traditional religious and mythical frameworks which have striven to reveal something of this same transcendent human potential. The interior monolog provided here is close to the experience of ecstasy recorded by Christian saints in their union with God. It reaches its absurd extreme in the later hallucinatory novel, *Barefoot in the Head*.

In this instance, Gren returns to normal reality because the transformation he nearly undergoes is reserved for the mindless vegetal forms which fill the *Hothouse* Earth. Nonetheless, the experience makes a deep and abiding impression and colors the rest of the book: "Finally to reach the infinite immensity of being nothing. . .the infinite richness of non-existence. . . and thus of becoming God. . . and thus of being the top and tail of one's own creation. . ." Head and tail, beginning and end, past and future: the extremes are shown not as opposites, but as identities in the cyclical process of creative change, a process which is Aldiss's bedrock of belief. It is a faith which affirms the christian paradox that "in my end is my beginning."

The identity of beginning and end is a part of the heat and cold imagery running through the novel. Temperature is, of course, a natural function of setting and environment, and something one could expect to find in practically any story by Aldiss; from *Equator* onward, however, temperature becomes a particularly important factor. Even the title, *Hothouse*, proclaims the importance to Aldiss of this imagery.

Leaving the island of the magic cliff, Gren's boat drifts further and further toward the dark side of the unmoving planet, toward the land of eternal night. Here, for the first time in their lives, they encounter ice, in the form of an iceberg. The tummy-bellies, whose quaint and picturesque speech patterns add a pleasant linguistic dimension to the style of the novel, exclaim from fear and ignorance, "Oh, oh, our death moment come hot upon us, ice cold in these nasty freezing jaws." The same hot-cold contrast is evident during another effort at escape, when they try to return from the dark side to the light, following the amazing stalker plants. Here the images are linked to beginnings and ends: "This sodden ruin in the middle of snow was at once the end and the beginning of the stalker plant's journey. Forced like all plants to solve the terrible problem of overcrowding in a hothouse world, it had done so by venturing into those chilly realms beyond the timberline where the jungle could not grow." The stalkers are part of an "unending cycle of life," and "continue the endless vegetable mode of being." The impression on Gren himself, however, forms a part of his growing consciousness, and contributes both physically and metaphorically to his journey. There is an echo here of Blake, who in the spiral from innocence through experience to higher innocence, observed that "without contraries there can be no progression."

Is *Hothouse* science fiction? The novel is short on outright scientific explanations, and there are mystical realms left totally unexplained. The appearance of the philosophical and priestly Sodal Ye at the book's end moves the fiction further outside the boundaries of science. Sodal Ye is more a prophet than a scientist, despite his considerable practical and scientific knowledge. Attending him are two disciples of the Arabler tribe, beings at once more advanced and more backward than ordinary humans. They have eschewed language and have lost the idea of passing time. Instead, they inhabit an undifferentiated "period of being," and are able to disappear at will to move forward and backward in time. They are described as "devolving" from human toward vegetative levels, and we are told that "to fail to distinguish between past and present and future needs a great concentration of ignorance." Despite such devolution, they have attained abilities and awareness which could, depending upon one's perspective, be considered more highly evolved consciousness. It is the Sodal Ye who recogni.es in the green streams from the planet, and the sun going nova, an apocalyptic message: "As I predicted," he cried, "all things are melting into light. The day is coming when the Great Day comes and all creatures become a part of the evergreen universe."

At the end of the novel, Gren is not ignorant of these realities. Realizing the inevitable apocalypse, he elects to live out his life in the home he knows. He will not seek escape, for he sees no purpose in it. "Go and good luck! Fill a whole empty world with people and fungus!" he tells the others. The morel calls him a fool for staying to face certain death by fire. "So you said, O wise morel. You also said that that would not come for many generations. Laren and his son and his son's son will live in the green, rather than be cooked into the gut of a vegetable making an unknown journey." Gren ignores the easy morality (morelity) of escape, and affirms his humanity "with a wonderful gladness in his heart." It is not simply a victory of heart over head, for though Haris says, "You don't know what you are doing," Gren replies, "That may be true; but at least I know what you are doing." The affirmation Gren makes is one which may well speak to all of us who live with certain knowledge of inevitable nuclear, ecological or psychic disintegration: "This shall be home, where danger was my cradle, and all we have learnt will guard us." At the end of this brilliantly conceived and skillfully wrought novel of fantastic fiction, the house has become at last a home.

A GREY AND BEAUTIFUL WORLD

Preoccupation with death and a sense of loss mark the two novels Aldiss published in 1964 though neither of them matches the breadth of vision or mythic stature of *Hothouse*. *The Dark Light-Years* reflects in its title the dark-light contrasts which were present in *Hothouse*; the effort to identify these contraries is one of the central themes of the novel. The utods are gigantic life forms with complex technological achievements, and basic assumptions about life, reality, and philosophy very different from those of human society. Having populated several planets, they are expanding their search for new and hospitable environs at the beginning of the book. Each utod can live up to 1100 years. Such prolonged life spans are only one of a multitude of factors which have prompted them to develop completely unique philosophical and behavioral patterns. The utods feel no pain, have no concept of fear, and like nothing better than wallowing, rhino-like, in mud mixed with their own dung. Their appearance is totally alien: "The animal had two heads, each of which held a brain. The two brains together weighed two thousand grams—a quarter more than man's. These animals, the ETAs or rhinomen, as the crew called them, had six limbs which ended in undoubted equivalents of hands."

The perspective of the story shifts, reflecting several different points of view. We learn things from utodian characters as well as humans. The book begins on the planet Dapdorf, where earthling (or Earthlegs, as he is called by the utods) Aylmer Ainson has maintained an outpost, living as a kind of anthropologist and linguist among the utods for 40 years. Ainson has managed to learn a little of their whistling language, but he has only one sound orifice (his mouth) to mimic intonations from eight utodian openings. The screeches and whistles of their tongue reflect the mental and cultural complexities of the 850-pound creatures who fashion "a poetry incapable of paraphrase." Near the end of this first section, the mother utod observes that "Frequently there are several versions of truth," a remark which foreshadows the various perspectives in the rest of the book.

The main body of the novel deals with Ainson's father, who participated in the first chance encounter with the utods on the planet Grudgrodd (utodian for "mistake"). After some of the startled utods have been killed, Master Explorer

Bruce Ainson, insists that the creatures have intelligence and language. Then he discovers their mound-like, dung-filled spaceship. The differences between the two life forms are so extensive that most Earthmen cannot believe that the utods are intelligent. The differences are evident in a "religious address" given by a utod leader: "They lay and listened to the web of his discourse as it was spun out of his eight orifices. He pointed out how the ammp trees and the utods were dependent upon each other, how the yield of the one depended on the yield of the other. He dwelt on the significance of the word 'yield' before going on to point out how both the trees and the utods (both being the manifestations of one spirit) depended on the light yield that poured from whichever of the Triple Suns they moved about. This light was the droppings of the suns, which made it a little absurd as well as miraculous. They should never forget, any of them, that they partook of the absurd as well as the miraculous. They must never get exalted or puffed up; for were not even their gods formed in the shape of a turdling?" The eschatological imagery of the book is at once miraculous and absurd. While it seems ridiculous from our perspective, and partly absurd from the utodian angle, Aldiss clearly desires that the religious dimension be taken seriously. The captive utods are members of a priestly expedition, and the only sympathetic human on the spaceship is Ainson, "a religious man."

A significant aspect of the encounter, apart from the communication problems posed by such alien species, clearly has to do with man's attitude toward death. ("Tod" is the German word for "death.") The utods view it as a positive experience, in which one is dispatched to the next cycle of nature: they refer to death as "translation," which relates the change to language and communication. The initial meeting of man and utod focuses on death; the creatures' predilection for feces also shows a utodian embrace of decay or death; utods feel no pain, and the ultimate outcome of research upon the captured utods has the humans vivisecting them, studying the pieces of living flesh as they disassemble the creatures, attempting to tell from this cutting-up job something about the animals that they could never discover by unsuccessful attempts to cross the language barrier. The novel as a whole forces us to consider fear of death as a problem in communication.

One inevitable conclusion is that mind and consciousness (and therefore the highest product of consciousness, language) are molded by physical experience and cultural heritage. The title of the book refers to a phrase used to describe spacemen, but one which could just as easily be applied to inhabitants of any spaceship planet: "I know how the long dark light-years attract and mold an inflexible mind." Inflexibility of mind is revealed in this novel on both sides. There is stubbornness by utod and Earthling alike. Individual humans actually fare pretty well, since at least they attempt to communicate with the utods; but the creatures are so wrapped up in abstractions that they cannot be bothered with inter-species communication. The central characters are the religious Master Explorer Bruce Ainson, director of the London Exozoo where the utods are taken, Sir Milhaly Pasztor (note the deliberate pun with "pastor"), and the son-missionary, Aylmer Ainson, with whom the story begins.

As any quick reading will show, communication is a central theme; supplementing this is the idea of relative perspectives. In one sense, all of Aldiss's work can be said to reflect a concern with perspectives. He follows the lead of Jonathan Swift's novel, *Gulliver's Travels*. Gulliver's visits to the tiny lilliputians and the gigantic Brobdingnagians are like microscoping and telescoping reality to achieve alternative perspectives. Actually, the utods are closer to Swift's Houyhnhnms, being more refined, intelligent, and happy than ordinary men. When Gulliver returns from his visit to the Houyhnhnms he finds that ordinary men make him sick, and prefers the company of horses, who remind him of Houyhnhnms. Swift has been accused of misanthropy on the basis of this one episode, and a similar charge could be leveled at Aldiss. Bruce Ainson, who like Gulliver has seen many new worlds and perspectives, muses: "You didn't go through the business of searching for new planets—with all the sweat and sacrifice that that entailed—merely because you hoped someday to find a race of beings to whom life was not just a burden for anyone with any sort of sensitivity. No, there was another side to that coin! You went because life on earth was such hell, because, to be quite precise, living with other human beings was such a messy job."

Aldiss acknowledges the mess, but never comes to hate all mankind for the difficulty of the task men face. In fact, the very choice to write science fiction and fantasy, rather than realistic fiction, reflects a desire to offer alternatives to current limited assumptions about nature and humanity. Toward the end of the novel, despite the inhumanity of the vivisection practiced upon the utods, the book promises, through the continuing presence of the fundamentally *good* Ainsons, the possibility of restoring the fresh and child-like vision of a world seen new. This, according to Lattimore, the spaceship's captain on its second mission, is something the "minor writers" were "fumbling to say last century before space travel even began." The excitement involved in achieving a fresh perspective/adventure/vision is what makes it all worthwhile—it's why the writers wrote the stuff: "Because this is the genuine and only thing, to feel the squeeze in your cells of a different gravity, to ride over a ground innocent of all thought of man, to be the first. . . it was like getting your childhood back."

But it remains for a woman to set the utods in proper perspective. The creatures possess both sexual characteristics in phases, being both male and female at various times in their life-cycles; humans still suffer the limitations of dichotomy, and since only the female part of the species can give birth, perhaps only the women can properly understand death: "You're all the same, you men," Mrs. Warhoon says at the end of the novel. "You're all cut off from the basic realities of life in a way a woman could never be. . . . all this fear of excreta—can't you see that to these poor unfortunate beings we have captured, their waste products are a sign of fertility, that they ceremonially offer their rejected mineral salts back to their earth when they have done with them? My god, what's so repulsive about that? Is it any more repulsive than the terrestrial religions where living sacrifices are offered up to various supposed deities? The trouble with our culture is that it is based on a fear of dirt, of poison, of excreta. You think excreta's bad, but it's the fear of it that's bad.''

At the end of the novel, its narrative focus returns to Ainson as he was at the beginning, living sympathetically among the utods after forty years of work to learn their language and understand their mode of life. He is comfortably awaiting his own death when his rescue arrives. Having earlier adopted the classic name Samuel Melmoth as a pseudonym to avoid identification with his father, Ainson has some difficulty remembering who he is when they address him as Melmoth, but he allows himself to be "rescued" in hopes that he can pass on some of the knowledge he has gained during years of work with language and communication. Unfortunately, a life's work is often "of no value except to the worker," since "the aliens were practically extinct, eradicated by the hazards of war." The normal Earthlings find themselves incapable of understanding Ainson's contact with the utods, and can only regard his bizarre 40-year exile as a curiosity. Aldiss, who loves to poke fun at fellow author Robert Heinlein, can't resist taking a punch at this superficial attitude, using a Heinleinian word from *Stranger in a Strange Land*, and satirizing its popularity by equating it with rock band groupies: "How the grokkies would lap up the story!"

In the final paragraphs of his novel, Aldiss suggests that the oppressed and misunderstood utods might well beat man at his own game, turning the death-dealing weapons of man against him: "The younger one moved into the deserted building. He examined the armory. The soldiers had left it untouched. . . . He had remained patiently captive for a small fraction of his life. Now it was time that he thought about freedom. Time, too, that the rest of his brothers thought about freedom." This conclusion aligns Aldiss with the oppressed and victims of discrimination. It suggests that communication is the essential problem in understanding, that differences in life style and behavior and even physical appearances, are due primarily to environmental and cultural factors, and that by attempting to impose one's own cultural values and expectations upon another, one prohibits communication and denies freedom. Aldiss allows his utods the possibility of liberation, and simultaneously champions the cause of oppressed and misunderstood creatures and races facing extinction in a world we know all too well.

The threat of extinction looms over the entire human race, rather than any alien population, in Aldiss's *Greybeard*. Here, as in much of Aldiss's fiction, the men of the future have suffered the effects of globally devastating radiation. Though published in 1964, this novel is still valid as a commentary upon continued flirtation with nuclear weapons (the United States is presently moving forward with development of the Neutron Bomb, which will kill by radiation rather than explosion). The world of Aldiss's novel depicts a future inhabited by senior citizens, who as a result of radiation have lost the ability to reproduce. There are no children. In addition, civilization has moved rapidly backward (another trend many observers see in American society today). Man has entered a second period of superstition and conflict in Aldiss's world, similar in many respects to the Dark Ages.

The book begins with a chapter titled "The River: Sparcot." The river is an important motif in the novel, and, in the tradition of Thomas Hardy, the landscape itself takes on the presence of a character in the fiction. The first sentence provides an image of the cyclical endurance of nature, and gives a picture of regeneration and fertility in striking contrast to the aged and sterile world we are about to enter: "Through broken reeds the creature moved. It was not alone; its mate followed, and behind her five youngsters, joining the hunt with eagerness." And:"This had once been wheatland. Taking advantage of a period of neglect, weeds had risen up and had their day, choking the cereal. Later, a fire spread across the land, burning down the thistles and giant grasses. Rabbits, which prefer low growth, had moved in, nibbling the fresh green shoots that thrust through the ash. The shoots that survived this thinning process now found themselves with plenty of space in which to grow, and were now fair-sized young trees. The number of rabbits had consequently declined, for rabbits like open land; so the grass had its chance to return. Now it, in its turn, was being thinned beneath the continuing spread of the beeches. The few rabbits that hopped there were thin of flank."

Hothouse deals with a vegetal profusion of growth, and with human efforts to survive the overwhelming force of nature; *Greybeard* presents a strongly cyclical view of nature, a picture of secession, of changing domination, and a grand parade of dominant forms alternating with one another. Although the central problem in the narrative is that there will be no new human generation, the repeated images of life's revolving cycles suggest a force at work throughout the universe for renewing existence, one more powerful than whatever man-made forces may oppose the continuation of life.

The title character, Greybeard, is, like the surviving hares, "thin of flank." And like the rabbits who love the open land, Greybeard yearns "for a freedom beyond the flyblown safety of Sparcot." He is thrown in with the dull old people of the village, where time is standing still as the elderly remnants of the race wait out their days, constantly on guard against the outside world. The setting is full of symbolic images, including "the clock that ticked noisily on a shelf" and "his wristwatch . . . battered old souvenir of another world. . . it had not worked in a decade." Time, of course, plays an important role throughout the book: "One of the characteristics of age was that all avenues of talk led backward in time."

Part of the *raison d'etre* for science fiction is to explore alternatives for the future. Particularly in *Greybeard, Earthworks,* and *An Age,* Aldiss depicts futures which look to the past, creating a two-way mirror—we look through one side, and the future looks back at us from the other. Greybeard himself reflects this Janus-like image of peering backward as he meanders onward.

Aldiss's message is conveyed neatly through the presence of the river. Sparcot is a village near Oxford located on the Thames. By choosing the enduring river, Aldiss brings the book literally home to his English readers. The backward-looking attitude is imagistically seen as a "fossil" by Greybeard's friend Charley, as Charley argues, "The idea that man can do anything useful about his fate is an old idea. What do I mean? Yes, a fossil. It's something from another period. . . . we can't do anything. We just get carried along, like the water in this river." "You read a lot of things into the river," Greybeard replies, half laughing, and he kicks a stone into the water. Greybeard's kick suggests that he will not be content to move along with the flow. As a matter of fact, he decides to utilize the river for his escape from Sparcot, and he rides the water throughout the book as it suits him. Greybeard shows clearly that a man can be a stone in the current, and still not be swept away by his fate.

Greybeard had been a scientist assigned to document and report the end of the world. When fighting had broken out, a series of mishaps had sent him moving. He had later sold his research truck for survival. His halt at the village of Sparcot "lasted for eleven long grey years." Now he pushes off with a few of his closest friends to journey up the Thames toward Oxford and London. To his friends Towin and Becky "this journey was just another hardship; to him it was an end in itself." Greybeard's attitude in the face of adversity, and his philosophical approach to the significance of his journey, is a key to Aldiss's own attitudes toward the many journeys of science fiction: "The hardship of it was a pleasure. Life was a pleasure; he looked back at its moments, many of them as much shrouded in mist as the opposite bank of the Thames. Objectively, many of them held only misery, fear, confusion; but afterward, and even at the same time, he had known an exhilaration stronger than the misery, fear, or confusion. A fragment of belief came to him from another epoch: *cogito ergo sum*. For him that had not been true; his truth had been: *Sentio ergo sum*, I feel, so I exist. He enjoyed this fearful, miserable confused life, and not only because it made more sense than nonlife. He could never explain that to anyone." Greybeard's escape from Sparcot is based on his assumption that a man must feel fully and experience widely to satisfy his nature; time and experience have stopped in Sparcot for Greybeard. "Only in one aspect was this an escape; like every escape, it was also a new test."

When he reaches Oxford, Greybeard is once more awakened to the possibilities of life. There are still remnants in the old university town of the lively mental life once housed there, and Greybeard rediscovers his old scientific vehicle. At first he decides to dedicate himself once again to "record the death throes of the human race." He labors to earn money to buy back his portable lab, but finally recognizes that serving the role of mere recorder of history is not dynamic enough for him. It will shut him in a dead end circle, "a materialist trap." With his wife Martha he sets off once more on the river toward London.

The London section is a flashback depicting the old life, when Greybeard and Martha had met each other as children on the outskirts of London, and watched the world change with the effects of nuclear war. The account is realistic in its portrayal of the individual human consequences of man-made cataclysm, and adds depth to the characterization of both Greybeard and his wife. As they continue their journey, they fall in with a faith-healing quack named Jinadangelow. He promises immortality through miraculous potions and cures, but when pressed by Greybeard, admits it is a hoax. Jinadangelow reappears further up the river as an evangelist, and apparently has found some children, a clue that new life actually does exist. Through him Greybeard comes to understand that because of the greed the older generations would feel for any surviving young people, the children must necessarily hide to protect themselves. Otherwise, they would be preyed upon by the vulture-like senior citizens. At the very end of the book, Greybeard and his wife find that the children have been masquerading in animal hinds, afraid of other humans, but able to survive in the woods. The couple ally themselves with a child, and a new future for mankind seems a distinct possibility.

The book includes some fine characterizations, especially that of Greybeard himself. And it explores in human terms what it would mean if one generation really were cut off from past and future alike. Greybeard speaks of his isolation in time when he sees men "as if they were all actors performing their parts against a lead curtain that cut off forever every second as it passed—yet as he spoke he was concealing from them, for reasons of compassion, the harsher truth that the curtain was also barring them from the second and all time *before* (i.e., ahead of) them." His concern for the subject is Proustian, and in some ways surprising, given the British tradition of attention to links with the past, and bridges to the future.

Not only does the book concern itself with the detailed geography and landscape of Britain, but it deals with the country as a whole. One important discovery in the book is that "you can't call this England anymore—it's reverted to God. It's his country now, and it's the better for it." Greybeard explains to his wife near the end of the book that in the long grey days, aged citizens can't blame their plight upon the world; they have brought it on themselves. Throughout the book the natural cycles continue, the past giving way to the future. Greybeard is alone among men in wanting to press on, and he recognizes that "man's the thing that's stopped, not death. Everything else but us—the whole bag of tricks—goes on unabated." It's a theme very similar to *Hothouse*, and reflects, perhaps, feelings of isolation that Aldiss experienced in his own life, as well as his perceptions of a depraved nuclear age.

Aldiss's preoccupation with death and alienation (with the goal of freedom as an antidote) seems to have been connected in some significant way with the break-up of his first marriage. Though he does not linger on details, he does speak of the "long shadow of exile" which dominated his life from the time he was sent off to boarding school at the age of eight, throughout the first marriage, and until his marriage to Margaret Manson in 1965. In "Magic and Bare Boards," he comments that after his marriage to Margaret, he was able for the first time "to realize myself; my writing changed in accord with the mysterious gear-changes which carry individual evolutions forward. With my first wife, no such recognition took place. Indeed, as that marriage was approaching the last stages of destruction, I said to a certain person whose business it was to know us both that one of my anguishes was that, while I felt I had a clear picture of Her, she had no picture at all of Me. This was confirmed. It is impossible to live day after day with a shattered mirror. Rapport is the sun of existence." The destruction of rapport in his marriage is mirrored in the destruction of the sun in *Hothouse*, and by the unregenerative alienation of old age approaching death in *Greybeard*.

Greybeard reflects a profound alienation based on personal experience, but it also carries Aldiss's familiarity with the landscape of England into a new dimension. The author himself is his own best critic in this regard: "Although I see my true strengths to lie in the short story field," he writes in "Bare Boards," "I have novels for which I cannot but feel some warmth; most of them are involved with the portrayal of landscape." He observes that *Non-Stop* depicts figures swallowed up by their landscapes, while *Greybeard* merely places its figures in a familiar and reassuring landscape. Regarding *Hothouse*, he admits it is "a novel from which I always felt distanced, perhaps recalling the miserable circumstances under which it was written." Biography as a pertinent critical activity fell into ill repute with the New Critics, but Aldiss's remarks affirm that the artist is inevitably influenced by personal factors, whether they are the strains of a miserable marriage, or the affection for the land where one lives. Biographical details can illuminate the human dimension of creative work, bringing the imagery and symbolism home to readers who identify with the experiences of the author.

In a recent letter, Aldiss cautions against taking self-interpretation as gospel: "Don't trust entirely to a writer's comments on his own work. They are often creative rather than illuminative. Later one sees a different aspect." Still, the self-admitted preoccupation with landscape can be seen as an integral and affirmative part of Aldiss's fiction. One of the English writers he most admires, Thomas Hardy, constantly reminds us in his novels (*The Return of the Native*, for example) that the human being plays out the drama of life against the scenery of landscape. This landscape, like the life lived within it, can inspire love and fear, pain and suffering, sorrow and joy. "English writers exist in intimate relationship to landscape and use it instinctively as a way of expressing mood," Aldiss concludes in the same letter, "as I did in possible over-abundance in *Greybeard*." The abundance of landscape in the novel serves to balance and ground the uncertainties of a shaky human future, linking the unknown with the known in a concrete and poetic manner. It reminds us in concrete fictive terms that man is not detached from place. Individual discovery of an almost mystical connection with place can be the beginning of self-discovery as well as a basis for human continuity. The faces change, the land endures.

Aldiss's novel *Earthworks* (1965) explores landscape from yet another perspective. Based on a short story with a macabre pun-title, "Skeleton Crew," *Earthworks* begins with the strongest death images and feelings of alienation yet to appear in his published work. Cut off from any link with the land and nearly alone on an automated ship, the characters are hostile to one another as well as out of touch with their environment: "we were busy suffocating each other, in love and nerves, in sickness and familiarity." (The fact that the alienation is described in a paraphrase from the marriage ceremony may be another reflection of the author's first marriage). The first scene of the novel is unforgettable, as a dead man slowly comes toward the ship, apparently walking across the water. Religious implications are clearly mixed with the heritage of technology which forms part of the futuristic environment. Here is an apparent miracle which echoes Christ, but in Aldiss's tale, there is no resurrection; the dead man is horribly dead, and offers no hope of salvation. The book begins "on the day of this new dead man," and the personal associations of the book are reinforced by that fact that it is told in first person, making it quite close to the individual consciousness of its narrator, Knowle Noland. The name suggests uprooted and alienated knowledge: knowing, with no land to connect it or oneself to. The narrative style is full of pain and alienation. The voice is excruciatingly self-conscious, and aware of "the imprisonment words bring." The narrator is bound by his name, his knowledge, his head. He is imprisoned by his job—as narrator and crew member—on a vessel with a skeleton crew to look after the automatic macinery which does all the work, adrift on one of those "great grey ships sailing the seas and rarely touching land."

About a third of the way into the book, the narrator tells us about his experiences as a (forced) farm laborer, on land which man has practically destroyed through his ill treatment of the environment. The Farmer, his "warden," was a paper-shuffling executive who lived in the city; most of the work was done by machine, though there was "still plenty of work for humans, work often too dangerous for machines." During his work force days, Noland had discovered a ruin, "the corpse of a world where the individual had had some status." (Note the death—"corpse"—associations with this past.) Noland had stolen some books from a building there, and was returning for more when he was captured by the Travellers. Through a kind of hallucination, we are brought to the central focus of the book. "The Travellers," we are told, "represented some sort of initiative for the future in a continent full of *dead* ends" (my italics).

It is in this section that we begin to witness the resurrection of the book, a life-restoring creative practice of an ancient art: "You need courage because writing is confessing, and my biggest confession of all must come in this section. I love the Travellers, yet I betrayed Jess! . . . I have peformed a sort of resurrection of this ancient art form." The narrator becomes a vehicle for Aldiss to confess his inner instincts as a serious writer, attempting to build a vital literature in the 20th century, when the book has already become old-fashioned: "No way of solving these problems exists any more. The conventions collapsed like old bridges. On the one side of the gulf is the mind, eternal and untouched—on the other, the body, running, jumping, bleeding. Better to copy the method of the thrillers I find among old book piles (converted by the passage of two hundred years into the subtlest of all signposts to those old days of plenty), and stick to the body. The mind can take care of itself, as it has had to from the very beginning; it's not as smart as body, but it can survive. And when I cannot resist it, I will pop up and be my own editor and commentator."

In his selection of a literary approach, Noland picked as his primary one the journey archetype which has run from Odysseus to the Time Traveller. But one cannot actually become a Traveller until one has been sterilized; "A pregnancy was as good as a death sentence to a travelling woman." To be merely a traditional Traveller for Aldiss (the writer) would be sterile and uncreative. *Earthworks* is a prelude to a period of new stylistic fertility in both form and narrative structure. Even its self-conscious narrator-without-a-country, subject to hallucinations which cripple and reveal his life, prefigures the hallucinogenic prose of *Probability A* and *Barefoot in the Head*.

The turning point in the novel occurs where Noland once again "recognizes the landscape," since his escape plan depends upon "this very strip of earth I plodded over." In the feigned madness which results in his capture, Noland falls "face down into the soil," as close to the earth as he can get. He is suddenly surrounded by "devils," the fire-throwing, automated night guards, and inexorably trapped. He is whisked off to an execution chamber, and Noland's captors demand to know the identity of the mythical hero "Jess." The Travellers stand united in refusing to reveal their leader, but Noland betrays them, and the whole group is destroyed. Nolan himself is taken away, carefully interrogated, and finally brought before The Farmer is a scene out of Kafka. He is scolded, given a job on the ship as a reward, and a cash bonus for his intended betrayal.

The entire flashback is presented as a kind of hallucination. At the end of it all, halfway through the book, we are back at the beginning on the bridge of the boat, *Trieste Star*, having just run aground, "I had been dissolved myself," the narrator tells us. And a few pages later, in a pit he has dug himself, ". . . the universe erupted. First it was light, then sound, then a terrible heat that shrivelled my skin. I died then, or if I didn't, I knew death." The freightor's nuclear engines have exploded. The narrator's knowledge is linked to the knowledge of death; he and Doctor Thunderpeck are the lone survivors.

The narrative is a type of picaresque, a series of linked occurences held together by common thematic concerns, common images, and the personality of the narrator. Highly episodic, it uses cinematic techniques in "fading out," and making associational "cuts" from one scene to the next. As the narrator struggles in the verbal medium, he feels the enormous difficulty of communication: "Immensity. That is part of my illusion; I struggle to express it in words. . . . I was aware of the being of the desert and the sea. I knew that on a planetary scale those two great creations were heaving with an activity meaningless to man." The stylistic technique of gradually and partially capturing fragments of a greater whole serves to convey the immensity of which the narrator speaks; it also develops a series of dichotomies and contrasts—desert and sea, fixed landscape and relativity. Increasingly, imagistic and thematic materials are thrown together into a context of hallucination, an uncertain sense of reality, an awareness of scale so immense that it is impossible to obtain a comfortable perspective; clear antipathies are difficult to discern. The infinity of exterior space is mirrored by an equally unpredictable and infinite interior space.

Illusion and reality struggle throughout the novel, perhaps personified by the mysterious "Figure" which haunts the narrator from the very first pages, and increases in impact as the book progresses: "From the Figure I drew something like the same impression of an immense process, relevant to me yet unfathomable. If that Figure was a product of my mind, how uncomfortable to know that in my mind too the unknowable things ground on." Aldiss at his most alienated, at his most death-preoccupied, has created a narrator philosophically and emotionally at sea, who desperately grounds his ship; in the vaguely sensed workings of the *un*known, the man whose very name is *Know*les finds a ground for belief. At the bottom line, ground level, in the soil-rich earthworks, Aldiss discovers an inexplicable but actual faith in the unknown. Here is a much more directly investigated version of the conclusion in *Hothouse*: "You don't know what you are doing," Harris tells Gren; "That may be true; but at least I know what you are doing," Gren replies.

The word becomes flesh (illusion becomes reality) when Noland meets Justine; he has carried her packet of love letters (which he had removed from the pocket of the dead man at the beginning of the story) having read them as a novel, and suddenly she materializes, taking him to a baptism (actually a bath) in her sanctuary (her bathroom is referred to by the narrator as "this exotic holy of holies"). With Justine he is caught up in a web of intrigue he only begins to understand slowly. "When I turned to look at Justine, I saw how thin and pale she was; instinctively I moved to take her into my arms. The Figure was there before me! He must have been hiding behind one of the trees." Shaken, Noland asks Justine who it was. "He only comes to see you when you are near death," she tells him. "I am always near to death. I hate all human life, and death is my ally." The real is once again dissolving in an hallucinatory cinematic wash: "I threw myself on to the couch beside her. The couch immediately changed into a rough white surface, as if it too had died. . . I looked up. I lay inside a concrete pipe. . . . In me grew that weary sense of lack of identity that was itself an identification. *Non sum ergo sum*. I lay inside a concrete pipe. By being nothing,I am in everything." This paradoxical affirmation is another variation of a bedrock belief that "in the end is the beginning." It brings a new sense of identity to Noland. His recognition is manifest in physical form.

At the conclusion of the novel, individual feelings and belief coalesce with social and political philosophy. From the narrator's self-analysis, Aldiss extrapolates a certain amount of awareness. "My relationships with others mainly ended in failure or betrayal," Noland tells us. "What surer signpost is there to the failure of one's own personality?" But the observation is immediately amended, "I can see that the health of character is securely tied to the health of an age." Thus the hallucinatory and disturbed inner world is reflected in the chaotic and destructive outer reality. Individual failure and alienation are merely personal manifestations of an age which is "cut off" and incompetent. These correspondences become the focus for further development in *An Age*, (*Cryptozoic*), and *Barefoot in the Head*. Justine explains both levels at the end of the book when she attempts to describe political reality: "The current regime throughout the world remains almost unchallenged because there is nobody left who holds clear ideas about the nature of man and the universal character of the human condition. It arose because not enough people could command a metaphysical view of human nature. We are spiritually and agriculturally bankrupt—perhaps the two must always go together."

The novel ends in a temple, with Knowle Noland in control of death, and ready to administer it like a medicine. In another fit of madness, he confronts the mysterious Figure and recognizes it as himself. Through a pair of parables (one about sheep and goats, the other about the devil) Aldiss attempts to push his readers toward "a metaphysical view of human nature" so profoundly missing in the twentieth century. A series of reversals convinces Noland that only destruction on a mass scale—brought about in this case through war—can halt the cycles of human suffering and power politics. In a revolutionary image at the end, Noland "cradles" a rifle, hoping the death he can bring about will produce a human resurrection.

Earthworks leads its readers into a dimension of freedom, responsibility, and metaphysical depth beyond the grey and beautiful world which haunts the novels published in 1964 and 1965. At the end of the book, part of Noland's recognition concerns the defense mechanisms he has failed to recognize: "Until now, I had not realized that my ship was armoured; I saw that the grey of the street was nothing more than the shielding which covered almost everything, rendering us impervious to anything but a nuclear attack. As I clung to the wheel—we drove forward through the grey waters at a tremendous pace—it was hard to see our course, so thoroughly were the windows shielded." In this experience, all the external landscape is internalized to become a metaphor of self-knowledge: "From the ocean of myself, I knew something had evaporated." Noland gains something like self-determination: "What sort of phantom the Figure was, I still could not say; perhaps it has been my mind's projection of a wish to escape from my own wretched circumstances. . ." And after it is over he does not stop thinking: "But what did that mean, how had it improved me, morally, spiritually, physically?"

Earthworks succeeds in wedding the psychological and metaphysical realities in a convincing and compelling narrative structure which sets in motion new directions for Aldiss's SF. It faces the difficulties of language, psychology, and metaphysics, insisting that they should be a serious part of the science fiction writer's explorations. The voice of the narrator reads convincingly as a voice for Aldiss himself: "Philosophy is not my strong point, though I have tried many a time to make sense of my life, and of the killing drag of history, but I tried then to review the phantasies that my sickness had inflicted on me. Some I have set down in this narrative. At the time, they held as firm a place in my understanding as parts of the real world, and the continents of delusion which I had been forced to march were no more fantastic than Africa or England." As Noland waits with the rifle to kill the only leader able to preserve a precarious political order in the world, he is about to unleash the irrational forces of war; as Aldiss seeks to explore human significance amidst alienation, he is about to unleash the psychedelic forces of creative madness.

HEAD WATERS

Aldiss seems to have discovered intuitively an effective means of constructing longer fictions using associational blocks of related themes and images to link discreet episodes; since his *ouvre* is haunted by his preoccupation with space, time, and the individual consciousness, he came to the French *nouveau roman* with highly compatible stylistic and structural orientation. Aldiss resolved "I would cleanse my prose of its antiquities," he tells us in "Bare Boards." And the lessons he learned from novels by Michel Butor (especially *Passing*

Time) and Alain Robbe-Grillet were supplemented by film: "I admired their scrapping of many literary cliches. I was attracted by the way that Robbe-Grillet and Duras translated readily into cinematic terms. In particular, I was stunned by the Robbe-Grillet-Resnais film, *L'Anee Derniere a Marienbad,* with its temporal confusions, mysterious agonies, and alien perspectives. It still embodies for me many of the things I set most store by in SF while many other valuables are to be found in Luis Bunuel's recent film *Le Charme Discret de la Bourgeoisie.*"

It's not surprising that *Earthworks* should serve as such an effective transitional piece for the group of novels which follow. *Earthworks* (1965) and *An Age* (*Cryptozoic*) (1967) published before *Report on Probability A*, were both written after it. *Report*, which wasn't published until 1968, was written in 1962; the short story "Skeleton Crew" appeared in *Science Fantasy* in 1963, and must have been written close to the same time. Aldiss explains in a letter, "I fell for the French anti-novel, so-called. . . lean, hard-surfaced, non-mush-centered. I resolved to imitate them, or go them one better if possible. So before Margaret and I drove off for our year in Jugoslavia, I wrote *Report on Probability A*. Faber turned it down flat, wouldn't look at it. Only when Mike Moorcock kicked out the old gang and took over *New Worlds* did the ms. get printed. After that Faber embraced it with glee." Each of the novels shares a cerebral focus ("non-mush-centered"), an atmosphere of uncertainty, and a sense of psychological indeterminacy.

After the rejection of *Report* by Faber, Aldiss must have questioned his fictional technique. This may account for his settling on a hero-artist for *An Age*, published the year before *Report* in 1967. Edward Bush, the protagonist, is the creator of widely-acclaimed artistic works, Aldiss tells us, "But his art (ha!) had brought him easy rewards too early—more because he was one of the first artists to mind-travel, he suspected, than because the public was particularly struck by his solitary genius, or by his austere and increasingly monochromatic arrangements of movable blocks and traps expressing those obscure spatial relationships and time sychronizations which for Bush constituted the world." Though Bush works with three-dimensional sculptural materials, his kinship with the author seems clear. From the opening of the novel, Bush thinks he is "finished as an artist." Whether or not this reflects Aldiss's own attitude, the solution which Bush settles upon is close to the reversal of dichotomy which Aldiss explores in his fiction. Bush/Aldiss determines in the opening pages that "instead of dragging that load of externals inward, he would push the internals outward, related to macro-cosmic time." Time, a preoccupation in all the novels, gains a new dimensionality in *An Age* (also called *Cryptozoic* in America). It becomes, in the tradition of Wells's *The Time Machine*, a medium through which one travels at will. Clearly internalized as an invention of man, time is recognized most clearly in this novel as a primary inner experience which structures the basics of reality: time becomes landscape.

In "Bare Boards," Aldiss describes the book as one with "landscape as surrealism," which is to say, time as surrealism. One thinks immediately of Salvador Dali's famous surrealist painting, "The Persistence of Memory," a hard-edged empty landscape with a jutting rock face in the background, and four clock faces prominent in the foreground. One bluish clock hangs limp over the edge of a brown rectangular form, and a third flops like a pancake over a distorted flattened shape on the ground which bears a vague resemblance to a disembodied human face. The fourth and final clock appears to be eaten by ants. This is the landscape of Aldiss's novel. It is no accident that Bush is an artist, like Aldiss or Dali in the twentieth century, cut loose in time. What happens to the artist when accepted attitudes towards this dimension flap and wave in his mind, unfixed, when the human consciousness itself is set adrift in time to experience reality as a ghost, a presence unable to touch or alter the time/space in which it sojourns? As Dali's painting suggests, a man's view of time affects the very reality of substance; as time becomes fluid, the conventional shapes and outlines of invented reality flow to conform to the shapes of whatever they happen to rest upon. This is the artist as ghost: insulated from time through words, the literary artist passes through time unable to touch the world physically, though his consciousness is there.

Time-warps and folds enhance the narrative pleasures of the novel. Bush, a master mind-traveller, is coerced into the service of the Mind Travel Police Patrol, and then turns counter-agent when he is persuaded to serve with subversives and revolutionaries. The twists of the adventure mirror the intricacies of time, and rational understanding assumes the aspect of theoretical gamesmanship, in which Aldiss shows himself a master, spinning and unspinning whole theoretical constructions of the temporal universe. It is interesting and appropriate to note the lack of technological hardware in this tale. *An Age* explores the abstract in concrete terms, and echoes the concern for a metaphysical dimension expressed in *Earthworks*. Essentially a theoretical and conceptual book, the novel presents a future society in 2093 becoming increasingly non-material, in both literal and figurative terms, as more and more people escape into the realm of mind-travel. The travel drug CSD is available on the black market, and the government loses control. Instead of relying upon the official institute for travel arrangements, thousands of citizens abandon their homes and apartments, precariously leaving in their refrigerators the requisite quarter-pint of blood and living tissue which will eventually enable them to return to the present. The economy collapses. The problem is largely a question of escapism versus purpose and intent, and like the artist-hero, this aspect reflects a critical awareness of struggle over the purposes of SF. As in some of Aldiss's earlier works, the people of the future look to the past, and only the Promethean force of revolution is capable of interrupting the cycle. Aldiss comes down clearly on the side of those who would utilize time travel and CSD for purposeful creative and intellectual growth. Bush is haunted like Noland by a spectral figure, probably the anima aspect of himself which becomes physically manifest in Ann. After journeys into the Devonian past, and glimpses of the very origins of life which evolutionary theory supposes, the characters dive even deeper into time, into the shaping period of the earth itself. Then, amidst a landscape devoid of life and filled with the primordial movements of Earth, man confronts the deepest assumptions of his intellect.

Plot summary cannot serve adequately to indicate the richness of this novel. The series of surprising theoretical and personal reversals at the end negates the tendency to think in both dichotomies and absolutes. Faced with new revelations about the possible misinterpretation of the flow of time (the distinct possibility that time flows backward), Bush's girlfriend Ann begins to call the whole thing madness, and refuses to accept the force of the new theories. "I'm just an ordinary person," she says. "I've passed thirty-two years happy enough with a lie." But the counter-argument sways both the reader and the characters: "Happy, Ann? Really happy? Not frightened at heart, aware as several generations ahead to the twentieth century have been that some immense and awful revelation was about to burst?" It is an echo of Yeat's famous poem, "The Second Coming," that resounds through Aldiss's climactic chapter, "When the Dead Come to Life":

> "Things fall apart; the centre cannot hold;
> Mere anarchy is loosed upon the world,
> The blood-dimmed tide is loosed, and everywhere
>
> The ceremony of innocence is drowned;
> The best lack all conviction, while the worst
> Are full of passionate intensity.
>
> Surely some revelation is at hand;
> Surely the Second Coming is at hand."

The revelation is at hand, the revolution is at hand: both are suspended in a kind of limbo. Bush in fact suffers a mental breakdown in the novel, in the chapter "A New Man at the Institute," and the pall of insanity falls over the whole proceedings. There is a distinct possibility that the only serious and creative travellers, as well as the serious and effective leaders, may fall as victims of madness, and be alienated quite effectively from having any real impact on the main stream of events. The conclusion of the book finds Bush and the inventor of time travel in a mental hospital; Bush is denied a visit even from his own father. The mental isolation inflicted there is more complete than any experienced in the displacement of time travel, because the romantic vision breaks. It gives way at the end to confusion and lack of direction, is buoyed up only by irony, humor, and "slouch," a peculiar comic sense which is the Aldissian equivalent of Black Comedy. (Slouch, which was introduced in *Greybeard*, will be more fully discussed later).

The use of this particularly individual brand of comedy culminates in Aldiss's word games, and in this case undercuts the serious dimension of the heroine. Despite her presumed emotional involvement with Bush, despite her fear in the face of conceptions beyond her "ordinary" mind, Ann winds up being part of a word-game rather than, or at least in addition to, a fully realized character. Bush is in a mental ward at the end suffering from *anomia*. When doctors deny his father the right to visit him, the old man must listen to Frankland's teasing:

"there are strange coincidences to be accounted for, Ann, Annivale, [Annie Veil?], anomia. . . Do you know what an amnion is? In addition to pointing these out, Aldiss includes many other forms: anima, anonymity, amonia, ann-age: An Age. When Bush's father is unable to get through to see his son, or receive any reassurance about the future, he begins to stammer; the omniscient narrator observes: "Language was breaking down," on the next to last page of the book. It is not simply language, but human beings and mental abilities that are breaking under the strain. We are left with very little at the end: the father's bent head in the rain, "the slight-figured girl standing watching under a tree, water dripping from her lank fair hair," and an uncompleted prayer: "O Lord, in thy infinite mercy. . . . " We are left with even language broken off.

In one of his candid and instructive letters, Aldiss comments, "It would not quite take the form I ideally aimed for. Bush has his breakdown. . . so the mind-travel is actual. I wanted mind-travel also to be part of his madness rather than an analogue of it (his mind is wandering. . .), and could not achieve it. . . . I think I had a bit too much fun with Ann/Annivale/anomia/amonia/amnion—it all went to my head and, in a moment of mad inspiration, I altered the title of the British edition to *An Age*, which is a silly little title!—less that of a novel than an anecdote." Even in explanation, the puns creep into Aldiss's writing and the language blossoms. *Ann*ecdote it is. And the narrator's voice, sense of humor, and delight in language at the end of the novel provide the only counter to the bleak breakdown. There are no guns and no potential revolutions this time around: the revolutionaries have lost control of their own minds.

Report on Probability A, read immediately after *An Age*, seems to turn attention to the hard, tangible world, almost in an effort to find some fixed points of reference in the midst of dissolving psychological and temporal realities. The novel begins with an inscription from Goethe, "Do not, I beg you, look for anything behind phenomena. They are themselves their own lesson." It then shifts to an opening segment, "Go Who Waits," which begins by attempting the most minimal statements, saying what things *are not* rather than what they are: there is no frost, no wind, no rain, no sun, no shadows. The weather, the atmosphere, "showed a lack of character." Objects are described in detail: window-frames, the couch, the back of the chair ("hubs of a cartwheel"), the shapes and textures hauntingly repeat themselves, echoing one another. "Some of these objects were connected directly or in a more tenuous degree with the passage of time. G's clock had been specifically designed to indicate the passage of time; it was his clock, . . . On its face, which formed a circle, were the arabic numerals from one to twelve and a pair of hands. The smaller of the two hands pointed at the lower lobe of the figure eight, while the larger hand pointed at the space between the nine and the ten. These two hands had been at these positions, maintaining between them an angle of fifty degrees, for a period of something over eleven months." Time is fixed within time by space—time fixed at fifty degrees for eleven months. The narrative echoes a similar shape, a tale within a tale, a structural technique used extensively in English literature from Chaucer's *Canterbury Tales*, through Shakespeare's plays within plays, to contemporary examples like Fowles' *The Magus*. The "Report" itself is contained within another frame, one in which Domoladossa and Midlakemela attempt to comprehend the phenomenon described in the report, where "the time-flow rate seems to differ from our own." They have assumed sudden "congruence" with the phenomenon they call "Probability A"; they are concerned to detect the humanity of the parties they observe. "They may *look* human, but they may not *be* human," Domoladossa observes.

The state of frozen time is immediately associated with art, as two paintings are described in detail. Both of them seem to be Pre-Raphaelite paintings, full of rich and ornate detail; the second is clearly "The Hireling Shepherd" by William Holman Hunt, reproduced on the cover of the book. The artistic assumptions behind Hunt's painting (and Pre-Raphaelite art in general) and Aldiss's novel are similar: each detail has an equal validity, the shapes echoing one another. In Hunt's work, we see the circles of the wine keg on the shepherd, the heads of the shepherd and his temptress, the round apples in her lap. Aldiss's consistent concern for artistic consciousness at the centre of his stories is here expressed in painting rather than in literature. Dali, whose surrealist influence was mentioned in connection with *An Age*, once remarked that his greatest aim was to paint like a Pre-Raphaelite artist. He referred to their precise rendering of detail and the equal focus accorded each element of reality. The technique rendered their paintings awkward in some ways, since sharp-focused clarity of each part works against the illusion of perspective. In traditional painting, camera-like "out of focus" elements in foreground or background give the impression of depth. The assumption of the Pre-Raphaelites, Surrealists, and of Aldiss, is that since we can not know which perspective is most valid or absolute, any detail must be as important as any other. The microcosm mirrors the macrocosm, following Blakean Romanticism with an edge of insanity and a touch of 18th century classicism (irony, satire, and wit); it is "non-mush-centered," and assumes the ability "To see a world in a grain of sand/And a heaven in a wild flower, Hold infinity in the palm of your hand/And eternity in an hour," as Blake writes in "Auguries of Innocence."

A result of this style is the impression of continual surprise at the sequence of recorded information. Facts are somehow detached from one another. Direct cause and effect associations are less important than the metaphysical relationships between events. In the next section of the book we move rapidly from a counter in a shop, to a door, to a poster on the door, to the circus on the poster, to the lions in the circus. Suddenly we are back to the door, and there is an uncertainty at first whether the door is in the circus, or in the shop, which we have nearly forgotten by the time we read about a "man bearing a tray": "Behind the counter of the shop was a door covered by a poster advertising a circus that had once appeared locally; the circus had a Dozen Huge Untameable Lions performing in it. The door now opened. Through it came a man bearing a tray containing breakfast." Aldiss uses this style not only in the sentence arrangement and style, but also in the large organization of plot elements, creating an effect close to the apparently heightened reality of hallucination.

"The novel flopped in the States, with nobody to speak up for it; over here, it survives, I'm happy to say, and has enjoyed several reprintings as a paper-back,'' Aldiss explains parenthetically in a recent letter. This may be a case of separating the sheep from the goats, the division of SF into "highbrow and low-brow" which Aldiss has forecast. Certainly in *Probability A* Aldiss shows him-self to be self-consciously in the "highbrow" category, but it is a false dicho-tomy which he himself regrets and tries to avoid. There may indeed be a separa-tion of sheep and goats, just as there is a sharp division between the shepherd and his sheep in Hunt's painting, and just as the discreet objects and detached actions detailed in the "Report" are divided from one another, but the echoes, congruities, nuances, and overlapping edges link them together. Aldiss is seek-ing a new kind of organizational device, carrying the associational structure one step beyond the loose narrative links of earlier works, always pushing the limits of connection, straining at the leash. Ideally, he will keep both sheep and goats in his audience. With a little effort, the book's puzzling edges can be got round. And the stretch of consciousness demanded to encompass the work is a healthy and expanding exercise. Yet, partly for lack of critical enthusiasm in the States, readers on this side of the Atlantic have largely missed the heady experience.

Aldiss has succeeded in creating an English novel as fresh in both style and conception as anything produced by the flurry of activity surrounding the much-touted anti-novel. His book is distinctly English, with dialog which approaches the fine ear of his gifted contemporary, Harold Pinter. And the careful render-ing of detail, which has so long been an effective device for lending reality to science fiction, is perfectly at home in this slice into parallel worlds. We con-front a hall of mirrors, a corridor not of time (as in *An Age*) but of probability.

Halfway through the novel, the perspective is still not clear. One has encoun-tered innumerable reflections, but has yet to distinguish the mirror from the image being reflected. One is led to conclude that certainty in these matters is not to be found. The circle of observers expands to depict watchers watch-ing watchers watching watchers: Domoladossa and Midlakemela are being watched by two Distinguishers on a hillside, who in turn are being observed by a group of men in a New York building. Part of the observation is being carried out by a robot fly. Joe Growleth turns to Congressman Sadlier, explaining, "Our robot fly has materialized into a world where it so happens that the first group of inhabitants we come across is studying another world they have dis-covered—a world in which the inhabitants they watch are studying a report they have obtained from another world." The congressman wonders if perhaps they haven't "run into some kind of mental reflection-distortion effect—hitherto unknown," and Growleth suggests the various worlds could be "phase echoes," but there is clearly no single preferable explanation. The congressman very nearly represents the reader when he concludes, "All we are after is facts. We don't have to decide what reality is, thank God!" As is usually the case with congressmen, however, he has missed the point; deciding what reality is is *exactly* what we must do. "When you've finished it," Aldiss has said of the novel, "it leaves you with something; and much of that something you have had to supply for yourself—so of course lazy readers dislike it." What we have to supply is a coherent consciousness, a point of certain reference in an uncertain field, and the task is indeed not an easy one.

The book, like life itself, is built up of interruptions. Experience is not presented in the single continuous movement one has learned to expect from the organized plot. Characters pick up a magazine, read a few paragraphs from a story, put the magazine aside and begin to do something else. The character known only as "S" is observing the tawney-haired woman in the brick building through a telescope, and turns aside briefly to read sections of an installment of a boy's serial, "The Secret of the Grey Mill." His reading is not executed in one smooth sweep, but interrupted by his observations, and even when he has finished the piece in the magazine, we find he has only mastered a fragment; it concludes "Do not miss next week's gripping episode." Again and again through both the form and the style of the story, Aldiss involves his readers in experience which is not smooth and continuous. The flow of time and the build-up of sequential observations are never allowed to create the illusion of coherence. Coherence would be an assumption of meaning, or absolute truth, and this assumption can never be allowed to come from the author here. It is left to the reader to supply it for himself, if he can.

There is one sense in which experience is continuous, however. Whatever verb tense is used, the consciousness Aldiss imposes on his readers gives the impresssion of continuous present-time. Every event, character and detail must be recorded, often with identical description, each time it is encountered. People move from one room to the next, and as they emerge into different space they must be described anew. They may or may not be the same people. In any case, we are rarely allowed easy assumptions of knowledge built up from past experience.

In many of Aldiss's stories, the artist has played a major role; in this tale, it is the artistic product—the painting by William Holman Hunt—which takes center stage. The Suppressor of the Archives, another observer observing observers, is listening to a woman in a trance, who in a sing-song voice is apparently delivering the entire novel aloud as a "report" to a jury, for what purpose we are never certain. In a central passage, two members of the jury, The Impaler of Distortions and The Image Motivator, argue over a proper interpretation of the painting, which has a reality in several different "worlds" of the novel. The Image Motivator presents a convincing case for the painting as "a psycho-dynamic drama of unresolved time," and further explains that "It embodies all the preoccupations of the Victorian Age, such as their attitude towards nature and the promptings of morality. It also embodies—demonstrates, perhaps I should say—their painful incarceration within time, with which they were unable to come to terms even upon a theoretical level." It is characteristic of Aldiss as a keenly perceptive critic of both visual arts and literature to make this casual but incisive remark about the Victorians. His pioneering critical study of science fiction, *Billion Year Spree*, argues that preoccupation with time is a primary factor behind the tradition of science fiction. After all, Wells's *The Time Machine* was not only the first really modern science fiction novel, it also was the first direct suggestion that technology could dissolve the barriers of time. We have already seen in Aldiss's work how seriously he treats the temporal dimensions. The subtlety and fluidity of dimension in his fiction shows how far he has come from the imprisonment he sees in Hunt's painting.

The Image Motivator elaborates his interpretation with an analysis of an esthetic of the age: ". . . their painters became masters of the Unresolved, of the What Next? instant: the dilemma, the unanswered question, the suspended gesture, the pause before destruction—or, on the other hand, the hour of disaster, nemesis, prompting a glance back at previous moments. Almost all the greatest Victorian pictures represent beings in a temporal structure that seemed at the time to admit of no escape; so the paintings are cathartic in essence." It is one of the many strengths of Aldiss's writing that his spokesmen cast new light upon the past. Here he offers a mini-essay on Victorian art history, questioning the connection or relevance of past to present and future. While different observers in the novel gaze across separate probability worlds, we are coninuously aware that time has a different pace and dimension in each. The Image Motivator conjectures that the virgin oracle's trancelike report is being transmitted to her from some other source, perhaps directly from the consciousness of some person residing inside the other probability world. The origin of the point of view presented in the "Report" is never known. One possibility, of course, is that it is being transmitted from the painting itself. And assuming that art has a kind of eternity about it, it represents a moment of frozen time. within which only a limited number of possibilities or probabilities can function. (These speculations themselves are at least as probable as several others.) At any given moment, all probabilities coexist in inexplicable relation to one another through time: "Time is of the essence here. Is not the whole report an account of the failure of time in that particular universe, the Marian Universe, as we might conveniently term it, just as we are threatened with a temporaneous collapse here? Is it not a fact that these people we hear about are rendered immobile, powerless—no doubt by time-failure?" Just what Aldiss means by "time-failure" is hard to say. The reader is left to construe his own meanings. But Aldiss clearly is attempting to embrace the past, sprinkling his books with insights and essays on various periods of history, while projecting toward the future. Within his own work he moves toward a liberated and enlightened time-sense which represents a mastery of the dimension.

Within time dimensions and probabilities already separate and discreet from one another, each world becomes a mirror of the next and of ourselves. The elongated passage of time causes us to amend our own temporal perspectives, and the great pains the primary observers take in the "Report" to get a fleeting glimpse into other realities reinforce the scenes Aldiss provides his readers (or Holman Hunt allows his viewers). The work of art is common to each probability. And within the novel, each set of observers is locked within rigid limits, bounded by the limits of man-made perceptual instruments. The mirror motif becomes explicit in the instrument "C" uses to make his observations: "Lying below the window on the floor of the loft was a home-made instrument. It was constructed of six cylindrical tins, each . . . pushed into the tin above it to form a tube . . . small tabs of metal pointed inwards, holding in place two mirrors . . . . At a certain point . . . he stared into the bottom of the tube.

42

Through it, he could see the reflection in the top mirror of a small stretch of street otherwise inaccessible to his eyesight." Why would anyone go to such great lengths simply to see something beyond his eyesight? Motivation is never explained. It seems based in some innate instinct, a Promethean urge to reach beyond the present. In any event, the view obtained by such stretching of human capabilities through man-made constructions is "So oblique . . . that it needed long study before it could be interpreted." The oblique angle of vision is what makes this novel as a whole so intriguing. There are images, impressions, symbols, and a reality full of detailed phenomena slowly unfolding in an apparently random order. There are only two natural events of any major consequence in the book: a cat catches a bird, an incident which seems to shake the fabric of time; and a rainstorm, which shows that the man-made structures leak, puddles and pools forming inside the buildings—a reminder of the limitations of man's constructions to contain natural phenomena, but no denigration of the phenomena themselves.

In one of the last powerful images of the book, the "Report" is following "C." The whole section is worth quoting, because part of the impression of the image on the reader is in the style of writing: "As he lit the cigarette . . . the flame illuminated a very small picture stuck to the roof above C's head. C cast his glance upwards at the picture. It was a coloured card found in a packet of tea, one of a series of twenty-four entitled Wonders of Nature. It depicted two snakes. One snake had caught the tail of the other in its mouth. At the same time, the second snake had part of the tail of the first snake down his gullet. The two snakes lay in a circle, their eyes gleaming; they were swallowing each other. C blew out a cloud of smoke at them." It is the image of the Gnostic Ouroboros, a version of the Chinese yin-yang symbol, which suggests a union of dichotomies, creation with destruction, and forms a perfect image for time. In Christian myth, the serpent in the garden evoked man's fall from eternity into time; after the Ouroboros image, C is left still "to gaze through the window at the blackness of the garden."

The narrative breaks off here, and suddenly the point of view shifts briefly inside the painting: "Nobody was near. The sheep could take care of themselves. Within his imprisoning hand, he could feel the doomed moth flutter. Her hand was raised towards it in a gesture of indecision.

"She waited.

"He waited."

With its Death's Head moth, the lap full of apples, and an image of the shepherd and straying flock, the painting resonates a reenactment of the fall into isolation and death.

"I still believe that *Probability A* represents a writer carrying out his intentions as closely as possible; the symbols, particularly the use of the Holman Hunt painting, work effectively," Aldiss argues in his letter. He explains some of his intentions in "Bare Boards" when he characterizes the central situation in the novel as "a situation charged with a drama which is never resolved. Moreover, I withhold the emotion involved, so that a reader must put in emotion for himself." The novel is a catharsis, but in a way unlike that claimed for

Hunt's painting—Hunt always painted in *too much* emotion if anything—this is a catharsis in which the reader empties both abstraction and emotion into the book, as the book empties details and phenomena into the reader's mind. Reader and book coexist very much like the Ouroboros image.

The circular image concludes *Probability A*, echoing the many circles of objects and phenomena within the story. What is referred to at one point as a "circle of vision" puts the perspectives in this novel outside one another, separate from one another, alienated from one another. The circle of vision in *Barefoot in the Head* (1969) does not allow us a multiplicity of probability worlds; instead, the circle tightens and we are alone and tripping in a single head. Published in *New Worlds* as part of "The Acid Head War" series, the novel was a timely and surprisingly convincing version of '60s consciousness. In fact, there are relatively few books which have managed to capture that reality—Tom Wolfe's *Electric Kool-Aid Acid Test*, Richard Farina's *Been Down So Long It Looks Like Up to Me*, Aldous Huxley's *Island*, and Samuel Delany's *Dhalgren* are among the best—but Aldiss's exploration of Joycean language and acid associations remains the closest thing yet to an accurate literary rendering of the acid head.

Barefoot in the Head (1969) depicts a luxuriant landscape primarily through its lavish use of words. The point of the book has more to do with how crowded inner space can be than with the infinity of outer space. Colin Charteris is the hero of the book—his name suggests a "chart" or "map," coupled with "errors" or "eras"—in other words, communication and time. At the beginning of the novel, he seems to encompass a bottom line of consciousness with no where to go but up, a state of mind reflected in *Probability A* when, in one variant version of the Hunt painting, we see a novel with its title visible, *Low Point X*. In typical Aldissian fashion, low point equals high point, inside equals outside, and the delicate balancing act continues. Following an investigation of world within world, like a nest of Chinese boxes, Aldiss has pushed through a bare world of phenomena into pure internal space, an exploration of subjective reality: "He needed a bed, company, speech. Maybe even revelation. He felt nothing. All his animating images were of the past, yesterday's bread." The Christian wasteland lurks behind his condition, echoing the plea of Yeats's "Second Coming,"—"surely some revelation is at hand." The bread, which in the communion ceremony would suggest the redemptive body of Christ, is now stale, "yesterday's bread;" all the images are of the past, and the past is dead. The first sentence of the book tells us that *"The city was open to the nomad."* Charteris has become a nomad, a wanderer, a modern Melmoth careening his red Banshee sportscar along the infinite turnpikes of Europe, but the choice of words also reflects the pun of its split components, no mad. This is one of the books which Aldiss says depicts "figures in a landscape," but it is a landscape which becomes increasingly interiorized. Even on the second page of the book, the reader finds it necessary to grapple with the contradictory realities of consciousness as he reads the opposite alternative that *"This city seemed closed to the nomad."*

There is a central focus on language, naming, puns, style in this book about schizophrenic landscape perception. Charteris has self-consciously chosen his name: "It's an English name, a writer's name." Charteris is writing his own scenario, though much of it is composed at the subconscious level. He encounters a woman named Angelina, and the conversation veers towards questions of ultimate moral concern: "Do you believe in God any more, Signor?" Angelina asks. "If you are really interested, I believe we each have gods within us, and we must follow those," Charteris replies. Angelina instinctively recognizes a trap in this: "That's stupid! Those gods would just be reflections of ourselves and we should be indulging in egotism to worship them," but in the course of the novel, Charteris himself becomes a sort of godhead. The reader is able to carry the warning about god as "reflections of ourselves" throughout the book, but during a great deal of the narrative it is difficult to remember that reflections are based upon the presence of mirrors.

Barefoot in the Head can be viewed as another response to the rejection of the *Probability A* manuscript. Its premise is the dichotomy to the earlier manuscript, in that no one in the novel is subject to "tedium," a word which could be easily applied to many of the characters in *Probability*. Victims of the Acid Head War have succumbed to the PCA bombs, psychedelic weapons concocted by the Arabs. The bombs administer a tasteless, colorless, odorless drug which dissolves normal mental states to the point where its victims are constantly beset with terror or with joy. Charteris, like the central figures of both *An Age* and *Earthworks*, is subject to continual fits of hallucination. Impressions of the no/mad state are given through stylistic implosion; convoluted post-Joycean puns and semi-punctuated prose conduce the run-on mind through run-on sentences. A key theme of the book is found in one of the flashes Charteris records early in the novel, "asking always of each moment was it eternal could one walk through the hall and walk forever through the hall." The question sounds a little like the static, prolonged temporal reality of *Probability A*. All of these bare outlines are provided in the first section, "Northwards," which we can also think of as North Words; directional combinations recur throughout, linking geography and language; and the playful style keeps words constantly in mind: "shoveled down into his uncommon core to find there ore and always either/or." Internal rhyme within the prose is only one of the poetic techniques used by Aldiss in the novel. The narrative is interspersed with poetry written by Aldiss in a variety of forms from contemporary lyrics to concrete letter arrangements. The novel is built up of increasingly fragmented and free-associated images which develop a schizophrenic sympathy in the reader who follows the wild rush of impressions.

The stylistic predecessor of this novel is Joyce's *Ulysses*. Aldiss has embraced stream-of-consciousness totally, and executes it here with diction and direction unlike either Joyce or Virginia Wolfe. The other strong influence is cinematic. In many ways, *Barefoot* is similar to *Probability A* in its "cutting" technique—a relatively flat, uninterrupted juxtaposition of images. The primary difference between the two books lies in *Barefoot*'s personality and emotion, both of which are absent from *Probability A*. One reflects a psycholgocial interior, the other a static exterior.

Charteris has emphasized that his is an English writer's name (Leslie Charteris, the creator of the popular suspense hero, the Saint). But pop hero slang
is suddenly taken seriously in an age of unfixed belief; entertainment is trans-
formed into hero-worship, and slang jargon is desperately grasped as "saintly"
revelation. The book documents the elevation of Charteris to savior. The
associations are Christ-like and delusory at the same time—Promethean and
Protean, if you will—and as in the case of any god-turned-man (or man-turned-
god) time enters the picture, because the future is foreknown, and therefore,
in a sense, already in the past. "They saw each other in a frost of violence
crystallised recognized—a thousand self-photographing photographs fell about
them on each a glimpse without its clue a fist a wrist a shoe a wall a word a cry
Charteris we cry we hear his voice cry Paradise. What crazed triumph as Charteris foresuffers in utter puzzlement but yet did he not already do it all in menace
of future hour." The future society after the Acid Head War is a desolation of
autobahns and wreckage, fast-paced travel and confused crashes in interior
space. Charteris becomes part of a rock band and is worshipped as a saint.
He, like Christ, is all men. His Angelina is being taken to "his place," which
seems less a physical location than "a new model for thought." Like most of
Aldiss's new models, its underlying purpose is the elimination of dichotomy and
the illusion of alienation: "It's not town, not country. You can't say which it
is; that's why I like it—it stands for all I stand for. In the mundane world and
France, things like art and science have just spewed forth and swallowed up
everything else. There's nothing now left that's non-art or non-science. A lot of
things just gone. My place is neither urban nor non-urban. Fuzzy set, its own
non categorisable category." The language is more eloquent, but the promise
is close to that made by the most idealistic of the '60s flower people. At base,
Charteris seeks beyond conventional cultural categories for a new version of
truth which will speak to himself as archetypal mass man. But the illusion of
revelation is accompanied by an isolation even more complete than that afford-
ed when communication is an imperfect possibility: all reality is compacted into
this single hallucinating mind: "we are in my brain, it's all me. The nomad's
open to the city. I am projecting. . . ." Charteris sees himself as God; imagining
the universe is complete solipsism. In *Probability A*, men struggled to perceive
reality through the clumsy circle of vision allowed them by the man-made universe; but at least one was left with the assumption that there *was* a reality
going on someplace else which could be observed. Here the world is a photograph of one man's head, in this case a moving photograph, which reaches overt
dimensions at the end of the book with the filming of Charteris's life. Despite
the high content of personality and emotion, some of the theory of the anti-novel
is still apparent: "Fiction to be mental photographs, motion to be supplied
purely by the reader," Charteris notes at one point. Yet Charteris is caught up
in a frenzy of motion, and the reader's real task is to slow him down and to distinguish true from imagined directions.

Great images of mass populations fill the pages of this book, and the world
condition is best symbolized in the giant superhighways, frequently depicted as
veins and arteries, and metaphorically as the blood vessels of the head we are

trapped inside. Charteris is in one sense a character lifted out of Kerouac. He is "on the road" a decade later, and though he is not Sal Paradise, the close resemblance between the two brings Kerouac's earlier fictional hero to mind. Aldiss speaks of the road with an updated jive, and one can sense the rhythms and blues influence of Kerouac behind the rock and psychedelic riffs of Aldiss's fiction: "The new autorace, born and bred on motorways; on these great one-dimensional roads rolling they mobius-stripped themselved naked to all sensation, beaded, bearded, belted, busted, bepileptic, tearing across the synthetic twen-cen landskip, seaming all the way across Urp, Aish, Chine, leaving them under their reefer-smoke, to the Archangels, godding it across the skidways in creasingack selleration bitch you'm in us all in catagusts of living."

Charteris is the self-proclaimed salvation of Man the Driver. He is hell-bent on recording the "appalling shawls of illusion draped across the people where the grey mattered." Yet the nomad on the super highway of Eurasia is at last not everyman, but "noman." The reader, supplying the motion, is bound to detect the rhythms of desperation, but none of the solidity of salvation. Angelina cautions Charteris against "either/whoring" and suggests that his promiscuity on both physical and mental planes rules out the constancy which might portend truth. But by this time the media have been brought in, he has become the larger-than-life Master, and his pronouncements, while self-indulgent, have a ring of truth. He has felt trapped by the "am/bushes of Westciv" (*cogito ergo sum; sentio ergo sum; non sum ergo sum*) on a treadmill going nowhere, where economics, politics, and philosophy have all jogged along with religion, pop culture, and mass culture. Charteris says the bills have all been paid: "Yes, the treadbill, trodden back to low point X and the city open to the noman. My friend, that was a short round we trod, less than two hundred degenerations the flintnapping cavesleepers first opened stareyes and we break down again with twentieth sensory perceptions of the circuit. . . . " This film is part of a circuit, a short circuit, connected to the neutral phenomenal universe of *Probability A*, and to a common image of art as a vehicle for shaping meaning in a confusing universe. However, the chaos of *Barefoot* tends to project itself into its internal work of art, the film, which is titled *The Unaimed Deadman*. Nomad has become noman has become deadman. The film depicts an old and new catastrophe, and suggests once more the refrain from Yeats's poem: "the only one sage, whistling under his breath the theme from *The Unaimed Deadman*. Things would fall apart this time from the dead centre."

The emptiness and horror of the global insanity depicted in the novel is believably extrapolated from the actual world. Though it is futuristic, all the seeds of these events are real and readily identifiable: speeding autos, the crashes of Man the Driver, competitive energy wars with Arab nations, psychedelic drugs, the tyranny of mass popular phenomena like film and rock music. This book accurately distills many of the concerns of the "freewheeling sixties," and reveals the dangers at the core of the counterculture: "That was the crux of it; they were all escaping from a state where the wrong things mattered; but they were now in a state where nothing matters to us." Angelina pleads for the film, the work of art, as a guide and mentor: "All the known world. . . loses its old staples and in only a few months everything will drop apart for lack of care. People who can must save the old order for better times before we're all psychedelic salvages and you in your film can show them how to keep a grip until the bombeffect wears thin." The film is no more reprieve than any other aspect of the schized-out world, subject as it is to images, actors, and the consciousness brought by the director, all of which are unequal to the task.

Charteris also remains inadequate to bring about salvation. He is washed under like all small men by the waves of forces far beyond his control. If he has become Christ, he will be subject, like Christ, to the human situation; and at the end, he is assaulted by fragments and disconnects: "At times he trod in every belief beneath a broken art sign or died again the thousand psychic deaths of croesus christs last autobile age." This is his mental crucifixion. "The brain still burned towards its wisdom," Aldiss tells us. Then he delivers fragmentary flashes of insight far from the coherence of wisdom: "Gigantic beast patient My ultimate wisdom my nonsense." With an image of apples reminiscent of the painting in *Probability A*, the ending goes a step beyond that novel. In the last section, "Homeward," we reach the point where *Probability A* ended ("They waited He waited") and are left with an observation which says almost nothing: "All possibilities and alternatives exist but ultimately/Ultimately you want it both ways." His tree becomes a shrine where tourists from the north can "stare and forget whatever was on their minds."

A selection of poems forms an epilog, and the final one, "Charteris," captures many of the qualities of the central figure.: "An ambiguity/Haunted him haunts/All men clarity/Has animal traits." *Barefoot* is a rich and extremely complex book, and cannot be completely delineated in this limited space. Another stanza from the same poem observes, "To some of us/They are unfinished/Palaces to some/Slums of nothingness." The book may seem like a slum or a palace: the reader must supply his own architecture. "It took me almost three years to write," Aldiss says of *Barefoot in the Head*, "and, when I'd finished it, I felt I had written myself out of SF."

FLASHBACK

What does a science fiction writer do when he finds he has written himself out of science fiction? The answer in Aldiss's case was to go back to where he had started. "I wrote ordinary novels instead," Aldiss explains. Returning to where he started, in "ordinary" fiction like *The Brightfount Diaries*, Aldiss produced two books which became intant best-sellers in England. He also completed a personal reminiscence, *The Shape of Further Things*, assembled the most comprehensive critical history of science fiction yet to be published (*Billion Year Spree*), and issued several collections of short stories. The period 1969-73 was a time for looking back to his roots, for reflecting upon the history and evolution of the science fiction genre, and constructing a personal memoir which helped put his own past in perspective. He had pushed himself beyond the boundaries of language, history, and genre, and it was time to retrench.

"Ordinary" is a word to be used in its best sense when applied to *The Hand-*

Reared Boy (1970); its recording of male rites of passage before the war is one with which any man can identify. The hero is Horatio Stubbs—a name which combines the sublime with the ridiculous—and in this readable and amusing novel, Stubbs comes convincingly to life. His history is continued in *A Soldier Erect* (1971), which follows Stubbs into the early 1940s as he joins the Royal Mendip Borderers, and is dispatched overseas to India. Stubb's battles are mainly for women, and the barracks humor is broader and more genial than anything Aldiss had written earlier. Neither of these novels has been widely read in America, probably because, as Aldiss says, "They embodied too British an experience." But Aldiss also believes "*A Soldier Erect* is probably the best of all my novels, shot through with pain and humour." Whether or not the assessment is accurate, these novels are significant in marking his return to standard fiction devices, without the aid of stylistic inventions or SF gimmicks. The author has thoroughly mastered the fundamentals of writing and the interlude in which these novels were written strengthened his mastery of the form. Horatio Stubbs is one of his most human characters.

In a letter dated June 15, 1977, Aldiss concludes, "Last night, at a fairly civilized hour, I finished the first draft of my third Horatio Stubbs novel, *A Rude Awakening*. Now I have the summer to rewrite and polish." And by the end of the month he reports, "the rewrite of *Awakening* goes well, but so slowly. I've just finished an early scene, very ample, set after dark in Margey's little shabby room. The funny thing is, I've held back on this novel vaguely for some twenty-five years and deliberately for some five; only now that I'm doing the second draft do I see that it is related quite closely to *Malacia*—closer than I really like; but perhaps readers won't notice. You never know what readers are going to notice." *A Rude Awakening* will perhaps bring Horatio Stubbs the audience he deserves on this side of the Atlantic; Aldiss plans a quartet, so there's still one more to go.

Also well worth more attention are the other "ordinary" books of this period. *The Shape of Further Things*, paraphrasing a title from H. G. Wells, gives us insights into Aldiss's widely ranging intellect, and suggests one basis for the projections of science fiction as they stem from the actual directions of the past and present. His history of science fiction, *Billion Year Spree*, is indispensable to anyone interested in the genre, revealing not only a wealth of information about titles and influences, but also giving us clues into the authors and styles which have most formed Aldiss's own writing. Each of these works shows the Aldissian preoccupation with time, drawing from the past, and projecting toward the future: time is a mine full of richness and sparkle, and the gems seem brighter as he brings them up from ever more obscure shafts.

There are not pages enough left in this study to explore these writings in detail. However, *Billion Year Spree* calls our attention to one historic work which serves as the basis for his next novel in a science fiction vein, and it's worth a brief look as a kind of precursor. According to Aldiss, Mary Shelley's *Frankenstein* is the first science fiction novel. She was able to utilize backgrounds of myth and magic to create her modern Prometheus, but she couched it mainly in terms of a growing scientific spirit, making it, according to Aldiss "the first great myth of the industrial age." Written before she was 20, *Frankenstein* shows Mary to be highly sensitive to language and feeling, and Aldiss finds one of the novel's greatest merits is "that its tale of exterior adventure and misfortune is always accompanied by a psychological depth," a remark which recalls Bush's effort in *An Age*: "instead of dragging that load of externals inward, he would push the internals outward." Aldiss explains in a note that Mary Shelley could well have said of her work what her husband said of his poetic drama *Prometheus Unbound*: "The imagery which I have employed will be found, in many instances, to have been drawn from the operations of the human mind, or from those external actions by which they are expressed." We have seen Aldiss's own explorations of the head and its imagery, and we can feel him strongly in sympathy with this aspect of Mary's writing, as well as with her delineation of what he calls "the two-faced triumphs of scientific progress. . . God—however often called upon—is an absentee landlord, and his lodgers scheme to take over the premises." Aldiss enumerates the book's primary themes in a succint and penetrating critical analysis of the book. He emphasizes man's confrontation with himself, caused by the disappearance of God, and the power of man's own creativity in making the new man; he admires her recognition of the precarious balance between old and new; and he is particularly concerned about the religious dimension. Perhaps this is the heavy burden born by any creator—one must supply meaning and morality for the creation. Bound by the demands of an essentially Romantic consciousness, Aldiss has pushed his moral touchstones to the limits of a single head, and wound up lost. By returning to the sources of SF in the Romantic tradition, he seizes again the essential threads of moral fibre which form the web of his work. His conclusions about *Frankenstein* in his critical discussion are expanded in his own Frankenstein novel, and are interesting as a prelude to it: "*Frankenstein* is a triumph of imagination: more than a new story, a new myth . . . . its effect as science fiction morality is no less powerful today than when it was written, surrounded as we are with so many fiends of our own designing. Yet it is appropriate that its closing words should be ' . . . lost in darkness and distance.' "

WHAT ROUGH BEAST

The words of Yeats's "Second Coming" circle through Aldiss's writing in implicit and explicit terms. His *Frankenstein Unbound* is a second coming of its own, resurrecting Mary Shelley's monster in a manner pertinent to the twentieth century. We have come around nearly to the end of this study, and near also to the end of Yeats's poem:

> "The darkness drops again; but now I know
> That twenty centuries of stony sleep
> Were vexed to nightmare by a rocking cradle,
> And what rough beast, its hour come round at last,
> Slouches towards Bethlehem to be born?"

The attempt to answer this question is the essence of *Frankenstein Unbound* and of most of Aldiss's writing. From the bedrock of English Romanticism, Aldiss has inherited the twin Romantic dichotomies of hope and despair. In fact, Shelley's own *Prometheus Unbound* speaks of this hope in terms reminiscent of the earlier portion of Yeats's poem:

> "The good want power, but to weep barren tears.
> The powerful goodness want: worse need for them.
> The wise want love; and those who love want wisdom;
> And all best things are thus confused to ill."

From the confusion of twentieth century nightmare, Aldiss looks back in *Frankenstein Unbound* to try to discover, then or now, the revelation at hand, and the nature of the beast which man has created.

Published in 1973, *Frankenstein Unbound* makes use of the layered perspectives which Aldiss explored as a narrative device in *Probability A*. Part One of the book is a short section composed of various documents—letters, a newspaper report, a cable, etc.—while Part Two is the taped journal of the protagonist, Joseph Bodenland. In other words, we are observers of an assembled report, and additional perspectives are provided from our knowledge of Mary Shelley's book, as well as the actual historical characters and incidents recorded. The first letter is dated August 20, 2020, which technically sets the book in the 21st century, but the numerous 20s suggest it is primarily a twentieth century document, and an attempt at 20-20 vision. The world is embroiled in racial warfare. Radiation from nuclear weaponry has interfered with the "infrastructure of space," causing a rupture in space/time. Timeslips occur unpredictably. A report from (ironically) *The Times* editorializes: "The Intellect has made our planet unsafe for intellect. We are suffering from the curse that was Baron Frankenstein's in Mary Shelley's novel: by seeking to control too much, we have lost control of ourselves." Bodenland, whose name places him firmly in the Aldiss mainstream, with its rootedness to "land" (the German prefix "Boden" means "earth" or "soil"), finds himself on the border of a timeslip and goes to investigate. Suddenly he is in Switzerland in 1816, at the time of Victor Frankenstein's fictional experiments.

Aldiss's repeated depiction of temporal breakdowns builds up a message. In *Probability A*, we learned that artists of the 19th century felt trapped in time; the 20th century artist feels time slipping beneath him. Bounded by future shock and historical awareness of an unprecedented order, the literary artist, particularly one influenced by T. S. Eliot's belief in "Tradition and the Individual Talent," finds that present-tense work is constantly subject to slips into the past or future. In this novel, Bodenland experiences a shock of recognition which seems similar to what Aldiss must have felt when he recognized Mary Shelley's influence in his own work: "I felt myself in the presence of myth and, by association, *accepted myself as mythical*!" Awareness of the fourth dimensionality of time makes the SF writer mythical, and imposes also the knowledge that his myth is both temporary and disposable, the lesson that

Aldiss says he first learned in a bookshop throwing out books: "Every dog has his day." But despite the fact that myths are discarded, they attain an existence beyond time. This mythic dimension, Aldiss argues here, accords both of these things to the author and his creation: the Shelleys have the same fictive or mythic existence as the monster. "One thing you see I had already accepted. I had accepted the equal reality of Mary Shelley and her creation, Victor Frankenstein, just as I had accepted the equal reality of Victor and his monster. In my position, there was no difficulty in doing so, for they accepted my reality, and I was as much a mythical creature in their world as they would have been in mine." We have seen how frequently Aldiss features artist or writer heroes. Here he not only presents Bodenland as a spokesman for himelf, but provides speaking roles for Byron as well as Mary and Percy Shelley. Yet he doesn't bring them to us on a pedestal, but rather as flesh and blood human beings. He advocates a broadly based literary appeal, and aims his work for a much wider target than purely academic or enlightened *literati*. The far-ranging appeal of *Frankenstein* is one reason for Aldiss's great admiration, and the artist-heroes he writes about do not represent an ivory-tower estheticism as in some of the work by Wallace Stevens or John Barth, but are solidly grounded (BODEN LAND) in the creative imagination waiting to be released in every person.

The ability to perceive oneself as myth, as Joseph Campbell explains in *Creative Mythology*, contributes substantially to one's psychological health, being roughly equivalent to a religious experience. Bodenland's encounter with the monster gradually moves him to the religious dimension, almost like the Ancient Mariner. Gazing upon the monster's bride-to-be, Bodenland admits, "My reaction to all this was not one of horror. For Frankenstein's researches I felt horror, yes. But confronted with this unbreathing creature surmounted by that frozen but guiltless female face, I felt only pity. It was pity mainly for the weakness of human flesh, for the sad imperfection of us as a species, for our nakedness, our frail hold on life. To be, to remain human, was always a struggle, and the struggle always ultimately rewarded by death. True, the religious believed that death was only physical; but I had never allowed my instinctive religious feelings to come to the surface. Until now." Bodenland develops a ground of faith resting on the bedrock of the Romantic tradition. "Victor's plan for this creature's coming resurrection would be a blasphemy," he realizes, "and to say as much—to think as much—was to admit religion . . . to admit that there was a spirit that transcended the poor imperfect flesh. Flesh without spirit was obscene. Why else should the notion of Frankenstein's monster have affronted the imagination of generations, if it was not their intuition of God that was affronted." Like Coleridge's Mariner, he experiences what James Joyce calls an "epiphany": "I fell on my knees and wept, and called aloud to God. . . . How often, in my past life, I had claimed that one of the great benefits the nineteenth century had conferred on the West had been science's liberation of thought and feeling from organized religion. Organized religion, indeed! What had we in its place? Organized science! Whereas organized religion was never well organized, and often ran contrary to commercial interest, ... organized science had allied itself with Big Business and Government; it had no interest in the individual—its meat was statistics! It was death to the spirit.

"As science had gradually eroded the freedom of time, so it had eroded the freedom of belief. Anything which could not be proven in a laboratory by the scientific method . . . was ruled out." Bodenland suffers a great sense of loss as well as a flash of joy at this recognition. He is attempting to communicate a nonverbal experience within the boundaries of language, and must resort to rational discourse: "There had been a time, early in the nineteenth century, in Shelley's day, where the head and the heart had stood a chance of marching forward together. Now it had disappeared . . . " Here is one explanation of the significance of the breakdown element in so much of Aldiss's fiction; breakdowns are almost always caused by a victory of head over heart (it is no accident that Frankenstein's first name is Victor), and one which puts several limits on the possibility of transcendence. Yet here, portrayed through a mythic literary encounter, Aldiss celebrates just such a transcendency. The final explanation uses literary rather than religious terminology: "What I experienced as I fell on my knees was a metaphor." Following this literary-religious epiphany, Aldiss, having condemned the triumph of science, lauds the terrible beauty of its power: "In his anger, he was beautiful. I use the word "beautiful" knowing it to be inaccurate, yet not knowing how else to counteract the myth which has circulated for two centuries that Frankenstein's monster's face was a hideous conglomeration of second-hand features. It was not so. Perhaps the lie drew its life from a human longing for those chills of horror which are depraved forms of religious awe . . . . I can only declare that the face before me had a terrible beauty."

The horrifying thing is that the creature has escaped, is out of control. What Aldiss portrays as a dichotomy of the head and the heart becomes threatening when the head pushes itself daringly into unrestricted dominance and freedom. Bodenland grabs his swivel gun and fires it at the monster. Unlike earlier heroes, he is not left waiting; he acts. In dying, the monster continues speaking in his own defense: "In trying to destroy what you cannot understand, you destroy yourself . . . it is because of our similarities that you bring such detestation to bear upon me!" As the monster speaks its final words, a fire rocket is launched, perhaps as a signal by one of the villagers, bursting over the head of the monster, offering a beacon oddly like the star of Bethlehem: "Before the lurid light went out, the monster at my feet said, 'This I will tell you, and through you, all men, . . . that my death will weigh more heavily upon you than my life. No fury I might possess could be a match for yours. Moreover, though you seek to bury me, yet will you continuously resurrect me! Once I am unbound, I am unbounded!' " Is this the second coming? The revelation? Aldiss notes that the word "resurrect" is "delivered with ferocity."

Bodenland succeeds in killing the monster a second time, but a return is part of the prophecy. He remains part of the cycle of doing and undoing which we have seen in Aldiss's novels time and time again. But he has shown us here a hero who has come through the psychedelic storm, weathering the slips of time, capable of recognition and of action. At the end of the book Bodenland stands on guard. "Sudden triumph and calm filled me," he tells us. Though at the end he is "biding my time in darkness and distance," the hero, for the first time since *Earthworks*, is in control of things, in possession of a consciousness beyond the cycle of head and heart. Both have been swallowed up in action as he, like Promethus, commands fire to change the world. We leave Bodenland stranded in time and heroic; and he reaches us past the timeslips—*we have his report.*

In destroying Frankenstein's monster, Aldiss is suggesting both the creation and destruction of his literary ancestor. it should be clear from sparse plot summaries that the novels of Aldiss are not neatly classifiable as science fiction; in his view of reality, there are spills and leaks. Within his own novel, he sets to rest his association with the history of science fiction, killing off the old beast to assure the survival of his own sensibilities. The point is clearly foreshadowed in the first pages of the book, when Bodenland watches the children burying a machine, Doreen's scooter: "The machine was eventually buried, and they walked solemnly round it to make sure the last gleaming part was covered. . . They came back to the grave time and time again."

Aldiss joyously resurrects old SF stereotypes in *The Eighty Minute Hour* (1975). In 1974, he edited an anthology called *Space Opera*, collecting some fine examples of an SF subgenre. He describes it in his interesting introduction to the anthology: "What space opera does is to take a few light years and a pinch of reality and inflate thoroughly with melodrama, dreams, and a seasoning of screwy ideas." He refuses to define "Space Opera" specifically, but nonetheless gives a good account: "The term is both vague and inspired, and must have been coined with both affection and some scorn. . . analogously with opera itself, space opera has certain conventions which are essential to it, which are, in a way, its *raison d'etre.*" One must recall how frequently Aldiss's characters, often artists or writers, are called upon to account for their own *raison d'etres*, coming up with various unsatisfactory versions of *cogito ergo sum*; here the conventions form their own excuse. "Ideally, the Earth must be in peril, there must be a quest and a man to match the mighty hour. That man must confront aliens and exotic creatures. Space must flow past the ports like wine from a pitcher. Blood must run down the palace steps, and ships launch out into the louring dark. There must be a woman fairer than the skies and a villain darker than a Black Hole. And all must come right in the end." By reducing the genre of his serious writing to convention format, Aldiss shows himself the detached observer of his own fiction. His own contribution to Space Opera has about it an amused self-consciousness, stylistic flair and dexterity, and a double-edged humor based in the comic multiple meanings of language. These techniques stretch the limits of style and genre with the same exaggeration and audacity as the cramming of 80 minutes into an hour.

The roots of this unique comic style lie in the early sixties, mainly in *The Primal Urge*, and also in *Hothouse* to some extent. It is given a very interesting name in *Greybeard*. There it's called "slouch," and delivered by a stand-up comic named Dusty Dykes, "an almost menacingly ordinary little man." Dykes says: " 'You'll see I've abandoned my old gimmick of not having a gimmick,' " after he floats in on an enormous dollar bill and climbs down off it to the floor. " 'It's not the first time this country's economy has taken me for a ride'. . . Dusty Dykes shook a cautionary finger. It was his only gesture. 'Smiling won't help it,' he said. 'I know you're all sitting there naked under your clothes, but you can't embarrass me—I go to church and hear the sermon every Sunday. We are a wicked and promiscuous nation, and it gives me as much pleasure as the preacher to say so. I've no objection to morality, except that it's obsolete.

"Life gets worse every day. In the high court in California, they've stopped sentencing their criminals to death—they sentence them to life instead. Like the man said, there's no innocence anymore, just undetected crime. In the state of Illinois alone, there were enough sex murders last month to make you all realize how vicarious your position is.' " The jokes are blue, the future is black, and the comedian relaxes in a casual slouched position carrying the weight. "Did you enjoy him?" one girl asks another. "Well, yes, I guess I did. I mean, well, he kind of made me feel at home." *The Eighty Minute Hour* doesn't make you laugh out loud, but it slouches through the grand issues and themes of all Aldiss's work, "slouches towards Bethlehem to be born."

There is a lushness to this book that is appropriate to opera, a lushness absent from *Greybeard, Earthworks,* and *Probability A*. He has thrown together characters like "Devlin Carnate" and "Attica Saigon Smix," outrageous women and ridiculous men, thrown them into gothic castles and armor and futuristic spaceships and holographic films. "Every perspective had a perspective encased within it," he says of the interconnecting rooms of a building men had once called "the Ultimate Structure." And the entire book is built upon this principle, multiple meanings of words and levels of irony contained in the comic perspective of "slouch." Within the Chinese boxes of perspective is an underlying grid of pattern—the conventions of opera and the exaggerated strains of its refrains—including a narrative perspective which seems more real than ironic: "I want to write a good old-fashioned novel, with no more ambition in it than to reflect pleasure and disgust in what I see around me." It is clear he has moved beyond the vision of the '60s: "Drug-dreams cover old ground, and look back; I try to look forward, to encompass new thought."

The characters within the book play word-games which mirror the games played by Aldiss in writing it, and their comments shed an interesting light on the book. Dinah Sorbutt becomes miffed and exclaims, "Oh your cruddy, nonsparkling complex complicated word-games! How I loathe them! The world disintegrates and we play word-games!" Her partner's retort is brief; if the whole world had been occupied playing these games, they wouldn't be facing the destruction that more dangerous games have brought about. This is a book of games: hide and seek, crossword puzzles, mating games—a great hodge-podge of spectacle and confusion. Aldiss seems to describe his own attitude in the halls of Monty Zoomer: "And in his dream brain, the dream went on, dark, cosy, and befouled like a bird's nest. But he had learned to take his time; before he sunk into artifact-dream, he would walk round his house, rejoicing. . . . " Killing off the monster with a literary coup, Aldiss comes up smiling and bobbing. throughout this book he includes song lyrics, like comic arias, which help balance the lyrics of *Barefoot*. The end of the novel is just what it ought to be: "The happy ending came screaming and giggling back from the Mediterranean, shaking dead fish and oil slick from its multi-coloured coat. They all burst into song.

Mike

When our names are forgotten, remember the point
Of the exercise—never conform! Smoke a joint,
Say a prayer, have it off, take a trip, do your thing:
The world's at defiance when pleasure is king!

Jack

Whatever the patterns that govern us all,
I'd rather have some life than no life at all,
And this is life's moral we're made to present:
Although predetermined, it can be well-spent."

REPAIRING THE FABRIC

In a review of *Malacia Tapestry* (1976) David Pringle observed it "is not a science fiction novel by any stretch of definition . . . One suspects that Brian Aldiss has been re-imagining himself recently, not as a 'science fiction writer,' not as a 'social novelist,' but as a grand English eccentric, out of Charles Dickens by way of Mervyn Peake." The narrator of the novel, Perian de Chirolo, is a young actor with a Cassanova image, bent on seeing his time well-spent. Malacia is a city of charm and poverty, magic and ignorance, with streets like a carnival, and a sky populated by flying people. The city is ruled by a Supreme Council, whose function it is "to protect Malacia from change." Chirolo is another artist-hero, an actor "arrived at the highest pitch of my art," who becomes the focus for forces of change and stasis, the central conflict of the novel, and perhaps the subsuming theme of Aldiss's work. Change is the force at the heart and head of individual personality, and is the main visible evidence of that phenomenon we call time; it is the aspect of life which prompts discontent and the desire for love, communion, and communication.

At the beginning of *Malacia* "slouch" has become a burden. The glib tone is there, but Chirolo is hailed as one bent under its weight: "You look to bear the cares of the old wooden world on your shoulders"; and Otto Bengtsohn, the stoop-shouldered carnie-type who claims to have invented a new theatrical art form in his Zahnoscope and plans "to change the world," is another major figure trying to push beyond the limits of "slouch." Bengtsohn hires Chirolo to perform in his new artform, a "joyous tragedy" which in a primitive photographic process can "mercurize" real life into magic lantern images (Mercury is the god of messages). In order to capture the players from real life, they must pose absolutely still for five minutes at a stretch. Through this tragi-comedy, Chirolo meets the wealthy Armida and falls for her and they later escape into a grotesque palace: ". . . it was like being trapped inside a zahnoscope, with long vistas of light and shade contrived by window and tapestry . . . . The men who built the place had been so baffled by topography that they had in some instances left a curve of staircase incomplete, or caused a passageway to double back upon itself in despair, or left a potentially grand chamber unshaped, its rear wall broken rock." Both in Bengtsohn's attempt to reinvent art, and in the lovers' rendezvous inside this incomplete palace of art, Aldiss prefigures central metaphors for the primary task he faces in his novel. Not yet abandoning the old structures of literature, it is not enough for him to stage mock opera; he seeks a new and varied tapestry which can embrace both the joyous and tragic aspects of life. "I wanted a song that would connect all things, the large with the small, the real with the ideal," Chirolo tells us as he reaches for a guitar later in the novel.

The forces of magic and belief are manifest in the novel in two religions: Natural Religion and High Religion. It is the natural religion which carries the greatest wallop, particularly when Chirolo gets involved in an orgiastic upper-class hunt of primitive ancestral animals. These animals, nearly extinct, are close to primordial forms—dinosaurs, pterodactyls and reptiles. "They say that those hunters who have slain the really formidable ancestrals such as the tyrant-greave or the devil-jaw believe at the moment of the kill that they confront beings of infinite wisdom." Chirolo experiences this first hand as he engages in a life-death struggle with a devil-jaw, finally killing the maddened beast, but suffering severely himself. As life slipped away from his beast, "The eyes saw me . . . they seemed suddenly full of benign wisdom, pity—no savagery there at all, just as some one had once said it would be." He saves the life of Armida and sends her away with his friend before he himself slumps "a long way down the river of pain."

The devil-jaw is encountered almost as a rite of passage stemming from the Natural Religion. It is linked through the "devil" of its name to the central tapestry passage of the novel:

> " 'Somebody told me that Satan has decided to close the
> world down, and the magicians have agreed. What would happen
> wouldn't be unpleasant at all, but just ordinary life going on
> more and more slowly until it stopped absolutely.'
> 'Like a clock stopping,' Armida suggested.
> 'More like a tapestry,' Bedalar said. 'I mean, one day like
> today, things might run down and never move again, so that we and
> everything would hang there like a tapestry in the air for ever more.' "

On the tapestry-hung halls of the lodge, where the aristocracy of Malacia hold their yearly hunt (a devastatingly satirical, enlarged version of an English fox hunt), and thereby uphold the tradition that prohibits change in Malacia as long as they continue "to slay the flesh of our Fathers," Chirolo finds himself in an orgy of madness, the people acting like "beasts in a jungle of the mind." He leaves for the hunt dimly aware of the repellent decadence of this ritual, and in the woods he encounters a Satanic revelation, "strokes of an infernal paintbrush," presided over by half men/half goats, proponents of the Natural Religion. Goats and satyrs are mentioned frequently in the book, but they play their most significant role in this scene. We have reached the place Aldiss spoke of when he mentioned casually that science fiction had reached the point where it divided into high brow and low brow, separating "the sheep from the goats." The shepherd was isolated from his sheep in *Probability A*; the serious religious vision moved with the satyrs to satire in *Eighty Minute Hour*. There is a further development in Malacia, where the satyrs are confronted squarely as creatures of evil; their parading of an ape dressed as a man is horrible and degrading to humanty: "To know them would entail total destruction. This intuition filled me with something more enduring than fear: recognition. The ancient wickedness about me became part of me, as I was a part of it. I choked on a dusty mouthful of recognition. Little different was I from the goat-lipped satyrs."

The satyrs question Chirolo, and he is unable to reply. "Until you have understanding of your nature," they tell him, "your errors—like the errors of history—repeat and repeat themselves in an endless fiction." This recognition scene continues for several pages, and is one of Aldiss's best passages. It combines fantastic occurence and possible hallucination or madness, with mystery, tension, a sense of danger, and high philosophical and moral concern. Chirolo gradually recovers from his fight, and comes away aged and *changed*. In fact, he has thwarted the changeless world of Malacia and of art. One of the Satanic satyrs speaks realistically as they impress him ("though whether in veritable words I could never afterwards determine") with the recognition that, "You must hope and despair, reform and sin, triumph and fail. How else do we live out our duality of spirit?" Afterwards, as Chirolo is recovering, a priest extends the advice, "In the continuing war between Good and Evil every man is little more than cannon-fodder. All we can do is to decide into which cannon we should allow ourselves to be thrust."

Chirolo completes his recovery with a visit to one of the greatest geniuses of the age, an elderly artist called Fatember, a painter of frescoes (a more permanent form of tapestry?) which he steadfastly refuses to complete. In their unfinished form, the great works can still reflect the changes of the artist, and Fatember's voice could almost be Aldiss himself as he explains why his vision is never complete: ". . . half of damned Malacia cannot comprehend on their life why I don't produce—why I don't yield up like a meadow, why I don't yoke myself up to my genius and get pulling until all is complete, my vision fulfilled. Well, for one thing, if I'm a meadow, I'm a sour one, over-cropped, never dunged. And if I'm an ox, I've been out to forage for too long, and no longer care for the rasp of the yoke on my shoulders. But if I'm a fool, that's different! Mayhap I prefer to leave the vision in all its glory where it retains its glory, inside my great wooden pudding of a head'—he smote it—'where the mice and merchants can't get at it . . . the truth is I care for nobody's wants but my own and God's when it comes to painting.''

At the end of the novel, Chirolo gives up his moral absolutism, and his insistence on purity of vision. He relaxes without neglecting the black and white dualisms of good and evil, love and hate. He finds contentment in a grey area in between; in the arms of another man's wife he is not alone: "The light of my candle, already diluted by grey shadows stealing through the casement, built a small enchanted landscape of the curves that made up her brows, her eyelids, her cheek, her chin. I tucked my arm round her and fell asleep.'' Perhaps the ultimate of his landscape novels, *The Malacia Tapestry* concludes with a human landscape, imperfect and ordinary, but flawlessly beautiful nonetheless.

In his interesting review of the book, David Pringle writes that "It is conceivably Aldiss's best novel, except that there is nothing else in the Aldiss *oeuvre* with which it can be compared directly.'' Whether or not it is his best is difficult to say, but this refreshingly different and masterfully-written book restates once more the depth and breadth of literary scope practiced by Aldiss, and is undoubtedly his best work since *Frankenstein Unbound*. It is only the first book of a planned trilogy, and augurs well for Aldiss's future.

Two other books still in galleys as this study goes to press are interesting, entertaining, and varied, but they lack the scope of *Malacia*. Readers will assume that *Brothers of the Head* is a sequel to *Barefoot in the Head*, but this is inaccurate. *Brothers* is a novella with a similar pop-culture setting; however, it differs in style and subject matter from the earlier book. The brief tale unfolds through reports given by the lawyer, lover, manager, and sister of Barry and Tom Howe, Siamese twins who are exploited as rock stars under the name of the Bang-Bang. In addition to the separate heads belonging to Barry and Tom, a third sleeping head lolls on Barry's half of the torso, giving the natural deformity an added macabre quality. Conflict in the story focuses on the violence between Barry and Tom—their only desire is to be apart, and at one point Barry even attempts to perform the operation himself with a carving knife.

Like a haunting tale by Poe, there is a lingering quality about the situation in this novella. The three-headed creature is psychologically convincing as a human being, and at the same time a physical incarnation of ego, id, and super-ego. The "sleeping" head, alive since birth in an unconscious and dream-like state, begins to awaken after Barry has suffered a heart attack. Doctors successfully implant an artificial heart pump, but brain damage has caused the head which was Barry to cease functioning. Tom, forced to carry both bodies around and managing to coordinate all four legs, only slowly realizes that he is being threatened with an even more deadly violence from the awakening third personality. In conception alone, the story is powerful, and the long monolog reports by the twins' lover, Laura Ashworth, and their sister Robbie, are finely rounded characterizations which simultaneously reveal plot.

Here again the landscape which gives its title to the book reflects the struggle for definition and identity. The title refers to the central character, of course, but in the story it is first associated with a piece of land, ''L'Estrange Head, a natural feature . . . . neither a true headland nor a true island. To determine its geographicl status under law, one would have to decide whether its baffling system of marshes, creeks and rivulets link it with or divide it from the mainland." The first glimpse of the brothers across this Head shows them locked together in combat, "punching each other steadily with a machine-like hatred." The brothers are a powerful metaphor for individual personality, as well as global politics, and are yet another example of Aldiss's struggle with problems of isolation, comunication, and conflict.

Last Orders collects the short stories published between 1973-1977, and reasserts Aldiss's expertise in the SF genre. In his "Author's Note," he describes a man in a "sharp suit" pushing his way through the crowd. He imagines the author as pianist at his typewriter, pounding out "the science fiction blues." The guy at the bar says, "Play something happy, something familiar," but the old piano man keeps right on with the blues. "See," he says, "my stories are about human woes, non-communication, disappointment, endurance, acceptance, love. Aren't those things real enough? . . . Change there will be . . . But the new old blues sing on for ever. . . " The guy isn't happy about this response. He tells the music man he should use his talent for "something positive," and he goes back into the crowd as the typewriter picks out its tune: "Everyone in the crowd was drinking fast, laughing and gesticulating. They knew the world was going to end next week."

Both the variety and vigor of Aldiss's writing, qualities which endure and mature with the years, argue against the world ending next week. He may write about it, but it's all part of the blues, part of the song, and the song goes on forever. To play a cheery polka would be false, though Aldiss admits, "I regret having no faith . . . more especially since I have lost hope in the idea of Reason as a guiding light." There is perhaps a kind of faith in the mere fact that the musician shows up again, night after night, year after year, playing those songs and playing them better, and making up new ones so we won't get tired hearing him play. His heroes and his art embody the resolution of Prometheus at the end of Shelly's poem, "To defy Power, which seems omni-potent;/To love, and bear; to hope till Hope creates/From its own wreck the thing it contemplates."

"Most of my opinions and emotions come in cycles, as does the weather," Aldiss says. "As a youngster, I mistrusted this apparent shifting sand of character: how disgraceful that one's opinions should change with the company. Now I have learned to live with and profit from the phenomenon." Like Prometheus, Frankenstein, or the Howe brothers, Aldiss will not be bound by convention; he constantly sings in his chains.

With the new and innovative stories of *Last Orders*, it would be fitting to mention a word Aldiss uses when speaking of his first stories in *Space, Time and Nathaniel*: "sprightly." He wrote prophetically in one of those early tales, "the start determines the resolution and the finish arbitrarily determines the beginning of the case." As he returns again and again to the themes, images and symbols which occupy his mind, his Protean changes in form and style catch the reader constantly by surprise. It was change which attracted him to science fiction in the first place—a fiction with more space for change. His later novels are difficult to classify within SF as a narrow genre; Aldiss will no

60

stay within neat boundaries. Chirolo ironically tells his father (a writer, like Aldiss, "whose opinions and emotions come in cycles"): "If you've reached the beginning of the world, your book must be nearly at an end." *Last Orders* has the freshness of a first book, and the wisdom of a mature author able to look back to the origins of time. It's hard to say where Aldiss goes from here. Perhaps T. S. Eliot comes closest in saying:

> "We shall not cease from exploration
> And the end of all our exploring
> Will be to arrive where we started
> And know the place for the first time."

BIOGRAPHY & BIBLIOGRAPHY

BRIAN WILSON ALDISS was born August 18, 1925, at East Dereham, Norfolk, England, the son of Stanley Aldiss (an outfitter) and Elizabeth May Wilson. After attending Framlingham College and West Buckland School he worked at a large variety of jobs, including outfitter, soldier, bookseller, art critic, and reviewer, before turning his full attention to writing. His first story, "Criminal Record," was published by *Science Fantasy* in 1954. Aldiss received the Hugo Award in 1962 for "Hothouse," and a Nebula in 1965 for "The Saliva Tree." He was also voted Britain's most popular author of science fiction by the British Science Fiction Association in 1969, and received a Ditmar Award as the world's best contemporary SF author in 1970. With his wife, Margaret, and his four children, Clive, Caroline, Timothy, and Charlotte, he lives a rural existence near the town of Abingdon, England.

1. *The Brightfount Diaries*. Faber & Faber, London, 1955, 200p, Cloth, Novel
2. *Space, Time and Nathaniel*. Faber & Faber, London, 1957, 208p, Cloth, Coll.
3. *Non-stop*. Faber & Faber, London, 1958, 252p, Cloth, Novel
3A. retitled: *Starship*. Criterion, New York, 1959, 256p, Cloth, Novel
4. *Vanguard from Alpha*. Ace, New York, 1959, 109p, Cloth, Novel
5. *No Time Like Tomorrow*. Signet, New York, 1959, 160p, Paper, Coll.
6. *The Canopy of Time*. Faber & Faber, London, 1959, 222p, Cloth, Coll.
7. *Galaxies Like Grains of Sand*. Signet, New York, 1960, 144p, Paper, Coll.
8. *Bow Down to Nul*. Ace, New York, 1960, 145p, Paper, Novel
8A. retitled: *The Interpreter*. Digit, London, 1961, 156p, Paper, Novel
9. *The Primal Urge*. Ballantine, New York, 1961, 191p, Paper, Novel
10. *Penguin Science Fiction*. Penguin, Harmondsworth, 1961, 236p, Paper, Anth.
11. *The Male Response*. Beacon, New York, 1961, 188p, Paper, Novel
12. *Equator*. Digit, London, 1961, 160p, Paper, Coll.
13. *Best Fantasy Stories*. Faber & Faber, London, 1962, 208p, Cloth, Anth.
14. *Hothouse*. Faber & Faber, London, 1962, 253p, Cloth, Novel
14A. retitled: *The Long Afternoon of Earth*. Signet, New York, 1962, 192p, Paper, Novel
15. *More Penguin Science Fiction*. Penguin, Harmondsworth, 1963, 236p, Paper, Anth.
16. *The Airs of Earth*. Faber & Faber, London, 1963, 256p, Cloth, Coll.
17. *Introducing SF*. Faber & Faber, London, 1964, 224p, Cloth, Anth.
18. *Yet More Penguin Science Fiction*. Penguin, Harmondsworth, 1964, 205p, Paper, Anth.
19. *Greybeard*. Faber & Faber, London, 1964, 237p, Cloth, Novel
20. *Starswarm*. Signet, New York, 1964, 159p, Paper, Coll.
21. *The Dark Light Years*. Faber & Faber, London, 1964, 190p, Cloth, Novel
22. *Earthworks*. Faber & Faber, London, 1965, 155p, Cloth, Novel

23. *Best Science Fiction Stories of Brian W. Aldiss*. Faber & Faber, London, 1965, 253p, Cloth, Coll.
23A. retitled: *Who Can Replace a Man?* Harcourt, Brace & World, New York, 1966, 253p, Cloth, Coll.
24. *Cities and Stones; a Traveller's Jugoslavia*. Faber & Faber, London, 1966, 291p, Cloth, Nonf.
25. *The Saliva Tree, and Other Strange Growths*. Faber & Faber, London, 1966, 232p, Cloth, Coll.
26. *Nebula Award Stories Two*. Doubleday, Garden City, 1967, 252p, Cloth, Anth. (with Harry Harrison)
27. *An Age*. Faber & Faber, London, 1967, 224p, Cloth, Novel
27A. retitled: *Cryptozoic!* Doubleday, Garden City, 1968, 240p, Cloth, Novel
28. *Farewell, Fantastic Venus!* Macdonald, London, 1968, 293p, Cloth, Anth. (with Harry Harrison)
28A. retitled: *All About Venus*. Dell, New York, 1968, 221p, Paper, Anth.
29. *Report on Probability A*. Faber & Faber, London, 1968, 176p, Cloth, Novel
30. *Barefoot in the Head*. Faber & Faber, London, 1969, 281p, Cloth, Novel
31. *Intangibles, Inc., and Other Stories*. Faber & Faber, London, 1969, 198p, Cloth, Coll.
32. *A Brian Aldiss Omnibus*. Sidgwick & Jackson, London, 1969, 508p, Cloth, Coll. [contains *The Interpreter, The Primal Urge*, and selected stories]
33. *The Hand-Reared Boy*. Weidenfeld & Nicolson, London, 1970, 189p, Cloth, Novel
34. *Neanderthal Planet*. Avon, New York, 1970, 192p, Paper, Coll.
35. *The Shape of Further Things; Speculations on Change*. Faber & Faber, London, 1970, 185p, Cloth, Nonf.
36. *The Moment of Eclipse*. Faber & Faber, London, 1970, 215p, Cloth, Coll.
37. *A Soldier Erect; or, Further Adventures of the Hand-Reared Boy*. Weidenfeld & Nicolson, London, 1971, 272p, Cloth, Novel
38. *Brian Aldiss Omnibus (2)*. Sidgwick & Jackson, London, 1971, 585p, Cloth, Coll. [contains *Space, Time, and Nathaniel, Non-Stop, The Male Response*]
39. *Best Science Fiction Stories of Brian W. Aldiss, Revised Edition*. Faber & Faber, London, 1971, 260p, Cloth, Coll.
40. *The Astounding-Analog Reader, Volume One*. Doubleday, Garden City, 1972, 530p, Cloth, Anth. (with Harry Harrison)
41. *The Book of Brian Aldiss*. DAW, New York, 1972, 191p, Paper, Coll.
41A. retitled: *The Comic Inferno*. New English Library, London, 1973, 159p, Paper, Coll.
42. *The Astounding-Analog Reader, Volume Two*. Doubleday, Garden City, 1973, 458p, Cloth, Anth. (with Harry Harrison)
43. *The Penguin Science Fiction Omnibus*. Penguin, Harmondsworth, 1973, 616p, Paper, Anth. [contains *Penguin Science Fiction, More Penguin Science Fiction, Yet More Penguin Science Fiction*]
44. *Billion Year Spree; the True History of Science Fiction*. Weidenfeld & Nicolson, London, 1973, 339p, Cloth, Nonf.

45. *Frankenstein Unbound*. Jonathan Cape, London, 1973, 184p, Cloth, Novel
46. *The Eighty-Minute Hour*. Jonathan Cape, London, 1974, 286p, Cloth, Novel
47. *Space Opera*. Orbit, London, 1974, 324p, Paper, Anth.
48. *Science Fiction Art*. New English Library, London, 1975, 128p, Paper, Nonf. Anth.
49. *Hell's Cartographers*. Weidenfeld & Nicolson, London, 1975, 246p, Cloth, Nonf.
50. *Space Odysseys*. Weidenfeld & Nicolson, London, 1975, 324p, Cloth, Anth.
51. *Decade the 1940's*. Macmillan, London, 1975, 213p, Cloth, Anth.
52. *Decade the 1950's*. Macmillan, London, 1976, 219p, Cloth, Anth.
53. *Galactic Empires, Volume One*. Weidenfeld & Nicolson, London, 1976, 338p, Cloth, Anth.
54. *Galactic Empires, Volume Two*. Weidenfeld & Nicolson, London, 1976, 296p, Cloth, Anth.
55. *The Malacia Tapestry*. Jonathan Cape, London, 1976, 314p, Cloth, Novel
56. *Decade the 1960's*. Macmillan, London, 1977, 287p, Cloth, Anth. (with Harry Harrison)
57-65. Aldiss has also edited the *Best SF* series (called *The Year's Best Science Fiction* in England) with Harry Harrison since 1967; the American editions are identified by date, the British by number.